TOUCHSTONE

MICHAEL McCARTHY
JEANNE McCARTEN
HELEN SANDIFORD

3

STUDENT'S BOOK

CAMBRIDGE
UNIVERSITY PRESS

CAMBRIDGE UNIVERSITY PRESS
Cambridge, New York, Melbourne, Madrid, Cape Town, Singapore, São Paulo, Delhi, Dubai, Tokyo

Cambridge University Press
32 Avenue of the Americas, New York, NY 10013–2473, USA

www.cambridge.org
Information on this title: www.cambridge.org/9780521665995

First published 2006
12th printing 2010

Printed in Hong Kong, China, by Golden Cup Printing Company Limited

A catalog record for this publication is available from the British Library.

ISBN 978-0-521-66599-5 pack consisting of student's book and self-study audio CD/CD-ROM (Windows®, Mac®)
ISBN 978-0-521-60139-9 pack consisting of student's book/Korea and self-study audio CD/CD-ROM (Windows®, Mac®)
ISBN 978-0-521-60140-5 pack consisting of student's book A and self-study audio CD/CD-ROM (Windows®, Mac®)
ISBN 978-0-521-60141-2 pack consisting of student's book B and self-study audio CD/CD-ROM (Windows®, Mac®)
ISBN 978-0-521-66598-8 workbook
ISBN 978-0-521-60142-9 workbook A
ISBN 978-0-521-60143-6 workbook B
ISBN 978-0-521-66597-1 teacher's edition
ISBN 978-0-521-66594-0 CDs (audio)
ISBN 978-0-521-66595-7 cassettes

Art direction, book design, photo research, and layout services: Adventure House, NYC
Audio production: Full House, NYC

Authors' acknowledgments

Touchstone has benefited from extensive development research. The authors and publishers would like to extend their particular thanks to the following reviewers, consultants, and piloters for their valuable insights and suggestions.

Reviewers and consultants:

Thomas Job Lane and Marilia de M. Zanella from **Associação Alumni**, São Paulo, Brazil; Simon Banha from **Phil Young's English School**, Curitiba, Brazil; Katy Cox from **Casa Thomas Jefferson**, Brasilia, Brazil; Rodrigo Santana from **CCBEU**, Goiânia, Brazil; Cristina Asperti, Nancy H. Lake, and Airton Pretini Junior from **CEL LEP**, São Paulo, Brazil; Sonia Cury from **Centro Britânico**, São Paulo, Brazil; Daniela Alves Meyer from **IBEU**, Rio de Janeiro, Brazil; Ayeska Farias from **Mai English**, Belo Horizonte, Brazil; Solange Cassiolato from **LTC**, São Paulo, Brazil; Fernando Prestes Maia from **Polidiomas**, São Paulo, Brazil; Chris Ritchie and Debora Schisler from **Seven Idiomas**, São Paulo, Brazil; Maria Teresa Maiztegui and Joacyr de Oliveira from **União Cultural EEUU**, São Paulo, Brazil; Sakae Onoda from **Chiba University of Commerce**, Ichikawa, Japan; James Boyd and Ann Conlon from **ECC Foreign Language Institute**, Osaka, Japan; Catherine Chamier from **ELEC**, Tokyo, Japan; Janaka Williams, Japan; David Aline from **Kanagawa University**, Yokohama, Japan; Brian Long from **Kyoto University of Foreign Studies**, Kyoto, Japan; Alistair Home and Brian Quinn from **Kyushu University**, Fukuoka, Japan; Rafael Dovale from **Matsushita Electric Industrial Co., Ltd.**, Osaka, Japan; Bill Acton, Michael Herriman, Bruce Monk, and Alan Thomson from **Nagoya University of Commerce**, Nisshin, Japan; Alan Bessette from **Poole Gakuin University**, Osaka, Japan; Brian Collins from **Sundai Foreign Language Institute, Tokyo College of Music**, Tokyo, Japan; Todd Odgers from **The Tokyo Center for Language and Culture**, Tokyo, Japan; Jion Hanagata from **Tokyo Foreign Language College**, Tokyo, Japan; Peter Collins and Charlene Mills from **Tokai University**, Hiratsuka, Japan; David Stewart from **Tokyo Institute of Technology**, Tokyo, Japan; Alberto Peto Villalobos from **Cenlex Santo Tomás**, Mexico City, Mexico; Diana Jones and Carlos Lizarraga from **Instituto Angloamericano**, Mexico City, Mexico; Raúl Mar and María Teresa Monroy from **Universidad de Cuautitlán Izcalli**, Mexico City, Mexico; JoAnn Miller from **Universidad del Valle de México**, Mexico City, Mexico; Orlando Carranza from **ICPNA**, Peru; Sister Melanie Bair and Jihyeon Jeon from **The Catholic University of Korea**, Seoul, South Korea; Peter E. Nelson from **Chung-Ang University**, Seoul, South Korea; Joseph Schouweiler from **Dongguk University**, Seoul, South Korea; Michael Brazil and Sean Witty from **Gwangwoon University**, Seoul, South Korea; Kelly Martin and Larry Michienzi from **Hankook FLS University**, Seoul, South Korea; Scott Duerstock and Jane Miller from **Konkuk University**, Seoul, South Korea; Athena Pichay from **Korea University**, Seoul, South Korea; Lane Darnell Bahl, Susan Caesar, and Aaron Hughes from **Korea University**, Seoul, South Korea; Farzana Hyland and Stephen van Vlack from **Sookmyung Women's University**, Seoul, South Korea; Hae-Young Kim, Terry Nelson, and Ron Schafrick from **Sungkyunkwan University**, Seoul, South Korea; Mary Chen and Michelle S. M. Fan from **Chinese Cultural University**, Taipei, Taiwan; Joseph Sorell from **Christ's College**, Taipei, Taiwan; Dan Aldridge and Brian Kleinsmith from **ELSI**, Taipei, Taiwan; Ching-Shyang Anna Chien and Duen-Yeh Charles Chang from **Hsin Wu Institute of Technology**, Taipei, Taiwan; Timothy Hogan, Andrew Rooney, and Dawn Young from **Language Training and Testing Center**, Taipei, Taiwan; Jen Mei Hsu and Yu-hwei Eunice Shih from **National Taiwan Normal University**, Taipei, Taiwan; Roma Starczewska and Su-Wei Wang from **PQ3R Taipei Language and Computer Center**, Taipei, Taiwan; Elaine Paris from **Shih Chien University**, Taipei, Taiwan; Jennifer Castello from **Cañada College**, Redwood City, California, USA; Dennis Johnson, Gregory Keech, and Penny Larson from **City College of San Francisco – Institute for International Students**, San Francisco, California, USA; Ditra Henry from **College of Lake County**, Gray's Lake, Illinois, USA; Madeleine Murphy from **College of San Mateo**, San Mateo, California, USA; Ben Yoder from **Harper College**, Palatine, Illinois, USA; Christine Aguila, John Lanier, Armando Mata, and Ellen Sellergren from **Lakeview Learning Center**, Chicago, Illinois, USA; Ellen Gomez from **Laney College**, Oakland, California, USA; Brian White from **Northeastern Illinois University**, Chicago, Illinois, USA; Randi Reppen from **Northern Arizona University**, Flagstaff, Arizona, USA; Janine Gluud from **San Francisco State University – College of Extended Learning**, San Francisco, California, USA; Peg Sarosy from **San Francisco State University – American Language Institute**, San Francisco, California, USA; David Mitchell from **UC Berkley Extension, ELP – English Language Program**, San Francisco, California, USA; Eileen Censotti, Kim Knutson, Dave Onufrock, Marnie Ramker, and Jerry Stanfield from **University of Illinois at Chicago – Tutorium in Intensive English**, Chicago, Illinois, USA; Johnnie Johnson Hafernik from **University of San Francisco, ESL Program**, San Francisco, California, USA; Judy Friedman from **New York Institute of Technology**, New York, New York, USA; Sheila Hackner from **St. John's University**, New York, New York, USA; Joan Lesikin from **William Paterson University**, Wayne, New Jersey, USA; Linda Pelc from **LaGuardia Community College**, Long Island City, New York, USA; Tamara Plotnick from **Pace University**, New York, USA; Lenore Rosenbluth from **Montclair State University**, Montclair, New Jersey, USA; Suzanne Seidel from **Nassau Community College**, Garden City, New York, USA; Debbie Un from **New York University, New School**, and **LaGuardia Community College**, New York, New York, USA; Cynthia Wiseman from **Hunter College**, New York, New York, USA; Aaron Lawson from **Cornell University**, Ithaca, New York, USA, for his help in corpus research; Belkis Yanes from **CTC Belo Monte**, Caracas, Venezuela; Victoria García from **English World**, Caracas, Venezuela; Kevin Bandy from **LT Language Teaching Services**, Caracas, Venezuela; Ivonne Quintero from **PDVSA**, Caracas, Venezuela.

Piloters:

Daniela Jorge from **ELFE Idiomas**, São Paulo, Brazil; Eloisa Marchesi Oliveira from **ETE Professor Camargo Aranha**, São Paulo, Brazil; Marilena Wanderley Pessoa from **IBEU**, Rio de Janeiro, Brazil; Marcia Lotaif from **LTC**, São Paulo, Brazil; Mirlei Valenzi from **USP English on Campus**, São Paulo, Brazil; Jelena Johanovic from **YEP International**, São Paulo, Brazil; James Steinman from **Osaka International College for Women**, Moriguchi, Japan; Brad Visgatis from **Osaka International University for Women**, Moriguchi, Japan; William Figoni from **Osaka Institute of Technology**, Osaka, Japan; Terry O'Brien from **Otani Women's University**, Tondabayashi, Japan; Gregory Kennerly from **YMCA Language Center** piloted at **Hankyu SHS**, Osaka, Japan; Daniel Alejandro Ramos and Salvador Enríquez Castaneda from **Instituto Cultural Mexicano-Norteamericano de Jalisco**, Guadalajara, Mexico; Patricia Robinson and Melida Valdes from **Universidad de Guadalajara**, Guadalajara, Mexico.

We would also like to thank the people who arranged recordings: Debbie Berktold, Bobbie Gore, Bill Kohler, Aaron Lawson, Terri Massin, Traci Suiter, Bryan Swan, and the many people who agreed to be recorded.

The authors would like to thank the **editorial** and **production** team: Sue Aldcorn, Janet Battiste, Sylvia P. Bloch, David Bohlke, Karen Brock, Jeff Chen, Sarah A. Cole, Sylvia Dare, Karen Davy, Jane Evison, Deborah Goldblatt, Paul Heacock, Louisa Hellegers, Cindee Howard, Eliza Jensen, Lesley Koustaff, Heather McCarron, Lise R. Minovitz, Diana Nam, Kathy Niemczyk, Sandra Pike, Danielle Power, Bill Preston, Janet Raskin, Mary Sandre, Tamar Savir, Susannah Sodergren, Shelagh Speers, Kayo Taguchi, Mary Vaughn, Jennifer Wilkin, Dorothy E. Zemach, and all the design and production team at Adventure House.

And these Cambridge University Press **staff** and **advisors**: Yumiko Akeba, Jim Anderson, Kanako Aoki, Mary Louise Baez, Carlos Barbisan, Alexandre Canizares, Cruz Castro, Kathleen Corley, Kate Cory-Wright, Riitta da Costa, Peter Davison, Elizabeth Fuzikava, Steven Golden, Yuri Hara, Catherine Higham, Gareth Knight, João Madureira, Andy Martin, Alejandro Martínez, Nigel McQuitty, Carine Mitchell, Mark O'Neil, Rebecca Ou, Antonio Puente, Colin Reublinger, Andrew Robinson, Dan Schulte, Kumiko Sekioka, Catherine Shih, Howard Siegelman, Ivan Sorrentino, Ian Sutherland, Alcione Tavares, Koen Van Landeghem, Sergio Varela, and Ellen Zlotnick.

In addition, the authors would like to thank Colin Hayes and Jeremy Mynott for making the project possible in the first place. Most of all, very special thanks are due to Mary Vaughn for her dedication, support, and professionalism. Helen Sandiford would like to thank her family and especially her husband, Bryan Swan, for his support and love.

Welcome to *Touchstone!*

We created the **Touchstone** series with the help of the *Cambridge International Corpus* of North American English. The corpus is a large database of language from everyday conversations, radio and television broadcasts, and newspapers and books.

Using computer software, we analyze the corpus to find out how people actually use English. We use the corpus as a "touchstone" to make sure that each lesson teaches you authentic and useful language. The corpus helps us choose and explain the grammar, vocabulary, and conversation strategies you need to communicate successfully in English.

Touchstone makes learning English fun. It gives you many different opportunities to interact with your classmates. You can exchange personal information, take class surveys, role-play situations, play games, and discuss topics of personal interest. Using **Touchstone**, you can develop confidence in your ability to understand real-life English and to express yourself clearly and effectively in everyday situations.

We hope you enjoy using **Touchstone** and wish you every success with your English classes.

Michael McCarthy
Jeanne McCarten
Helen Sandiford

Unit features

Getting started presents new grammar in natural contexts such as quizzes, surveys, interviews, conversations, and Web pages.

Figure it out challenges you to notice how grammar works.

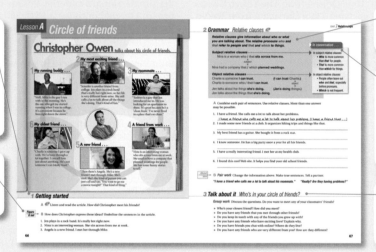

Grammar is presented in clear charts.

In conversation panels tell you about the grammar and vocabulary that are most frequent in spoken North American English.

Talk about it encourages you to discuss interesting questions with your classmates.

Building vocabulary and grammar combines new vocabulary and structures in one presentation, often to teach the grammar of a particular vocabulary set. In some units, vocabulary and grammar are presented separately.

Word sort helps you organize vocabulary and then use it to interact with your classmates.

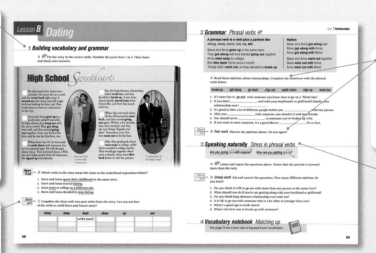

Grammar exercises give you practice with new structures and opportunities to exchange personal information with your classmates.

Speaking naturally helps you understand and use natural pronunciation and intonation.

Conversation strategy helps you "manage" conversations better. In this lesson, you learn how to use expressions to soften comments. The strategies are based on examples from the corpus.

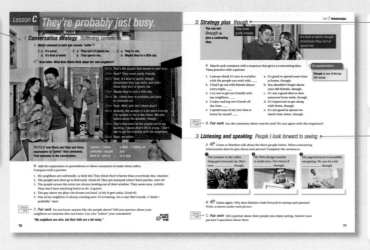

Strategy plus teaches important words and expressions for conversation management, such as using **though** to give a contrasting idea.

Listening and speaking skills are often practiced together. You listen to a variety of conversations based on real-life language. Tasks include "listen and react" activities.

Reading has interesting texts from newspapers, magazines, and the Internet. The activities help you develop reading skills.

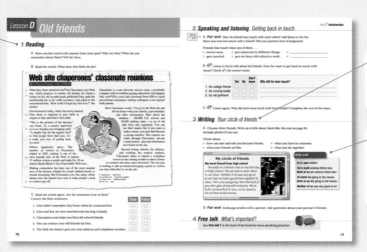

Writing tasks include blogs, reviews, letters, short articles, and reports.

Help notes give you information on things like punctuation, linking ideas, and organizing information.

Vocabulary notebook is a page of fun activities to help you organize and write down vocabulary.

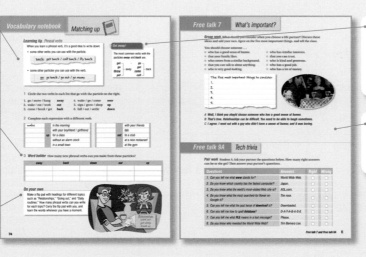

Word builder activities give you extra words and expressions to research and learn, allowing you to extend your vocabulary even more.

On your own is a practical task to help you learn vocabulary outside of class.

Fun facts from the corpus tell you the most frequent words and expressions for different topics.

Free talk helps you engage in free conversation with your classmates.

Other features

A **Touchstone checkpoint** after every three units reviews grammar, vocabulary, and conversation strategies.

A **Self-study Audio CD/ CD-ROM** gives you more practice with listening, speaking, and vocabulary building.

The **Class Audio Program** presents the conversations and listening activities in natural, lively English.

The **Workbook** gives you language practice and extra reading and writing activities. **Progress checks** help you assess your progress.

Touchstone *Level 3 Scope and sequence*

	Functions / Topics	Grammar	Vocabulary	Conversation strategies	Pronunciation
Unit 1 ***The way we are*** *pages 1–10*	• Talk about people's behavior and personality • Describe friends and people you admire • Talk about people's habits	• Manner adverbs vs. adjectives • Adverbs before adjectives and adverbs • Adjective prefixes	• Behavior and personality • Personal qualities	• Use *always* with a continuous verb to describe individual habits • Use *at least* to point out the positive side of a situation	• Rising and falling intonation in questions giving alternatives
Unit 2 ***Experiences*** *pages 11–20*	• Talk about your secret dreams • Discuss experiences you have and haven't had	• Present perfect statements • Present perfect and simple past questions and answers	• Past participles of irregular verbs	• Keeping the conversation going • Use response questions like *Do you?* and *Have you?* to show interest	• Reduced and unreduced forms of *have*
Unit 3 ***Wonders of the world*** *pages 21–30*	• Talk about human wonders like buildings and structures • Describe natural wonders and features	• Superlatives • Questions with *How* + adjective . . . ?	• Buildings and structures • Natural features	• Use short responses with *really* and *sure* to agree and to show you are a supportive listener • Use superlatives for emphasis	• Linking and deletion with superlatives

Touchstone **checkpoint Units 1–3**   **pages 31–32**

	Functions / Topics	Grammar	Vocabulary	Conversation strategies	Pronunciation
Unit 4 ***Family life*** *pages 33–42*	• Talk about gripes people have about family members and household rules • Talk about your memories of growing up	• Verbs *let*, *make*, *help*, *have*, *get*, *want*, *ask*, and *tell* • *Used to* and *would*	• Types of families • Relatives and extended family members	• Give opinions with expressions like *It seems like* . . . and *If you ask me*, . . . • Use expressions like *exactly*, *definitely*, and *absolutely* to agree	• Reduction of *used to*
Unit 5 ***Food choices*** *pages 43–52*	• Describe your eating habits • Talk about healthy eating • Discuss different ways to cook and prepare food	• Review of countable and uncountable nouns • Quantifiers *a little*, *a few*, *very little*, and *very few* • *Too*, *too much*, *too many*, and *enough*	• Containers and quantities • Methods of cooking	• Respond to suggestions by letting the other person decide • Refuse offers politely with expressions like *No, thanks. I'm fine.*	• Stressing new information
Unit 6 ***Managing life*** *pages 53–62*	• Talk about the future: plans, facts, predictions, and schedules • Offer advice and solutions to problems • Discuss phone habits	• The future with *will*, *going to*, the present continuous, and the simple present • Use *had better*, *ought to*, and *might want to* to say what's advisable • Use *have got to* and *going to have to* to say what's necessary • Use *would rather* to say what's preferable	• Expressions with *make* and *do*	• End phone conversations with expressions like *I'd better go*, *I've got to go*, and *I'll call you later* • Use informal expressions like *See you later* to end friendly phone conversations	• Reduction of *want to*, *you'd better*, *going to have to*, *ought to*, and *have got to*

Touchstone **checkpoint Units 4–6**   **pages 63–64**

Listening	Reading	Writing	Vocabulary notebook	Free talk
Best friends • Listen to three conversations about best friends, and then fill in a chart *I didn't know that!* • Match each person with a piece of information; then listen for more information about each person	*Five things you didn't know about . . .* • A magazine article with biographies of four famous people	• Write a short description of yourself • Learn useful expressions to include in a biography or personal profile	*Happy or sad?* • Learn new words and their opposites	*People are interesting!* • Class activity: Ask questions to find classmates who do interesting things
What have they done? • Listen to three conversations to identify the main topic; then choose the correct response to three comments *A traveler's adventures* • Listen to a conversation about a traveler's e-mail, and identify key information in the pictures; then listen and answer questions about the details	*Greetings from the Galápagos* and *I'm in Athens!* • Two travel blogs	• Write a blog describing an exciting experience • Use adverbs like *fortunately*, *unfortunately*, and *amazingly* to show your attitude or feeling	*Have you ever . . . ?* • Write the three main forms of different verbs in charts	*Can you believe it? I've never done that!* • Group game: Each person fills out a chart; then group members compare answers and score points
What do you know? • Take a quiz; then listen to a quiz show to check your answers and answer questions *Travel talk* • Listen to a radio interview, and number photos in order; then listen and answer questions about the details	*World records* • Fascinating facts from a book of world records	• Write a paragraph about a human or natural wonder in your country • Add information about a place or thing	*From the mountains to the sea* • Draw and label a map to remember the vocabulary of natural features, buildings, and structures	*The five greatest wonders* • Group work: Choose and rank your country's five greatest wonders; then compare lists with the class

Touchstone **checkpoint Units 1–3** **pages 31–32**

Listening	Reading	Writing	Vocabulary notebook	Free talk
Reasonable demands? • Match each person with a parental demand; then listen and check your answers *Family activities* • Listen to three people describe their memories, and number the pictures in order; then listen again for more information	*Rhonda's Ramblings* • A blog recounting a girl's childhood experiences riding in the car with her brother	• Write a blog about a memory from your childhood • Use past and present time markers	*Remember that?* • Use word webs to log new vocabulary about family members	*Family histories* • Group work: Prepare a short history of your family; then present your history to the group
That sounds good. • Listen to conversations, and number pictures in order; then match each picture with the best response *Snack habits* • Listen to people talk about snacks, and number the pictures; then listen for details to complete a chart	*Popular snacks around the world* • A magazine article about five popular snack foods	• Write a short article about a snack food or traditional dish for a tourist pamphlet • Introduce examples with *like, for example,* and *such as*	*Fried bananas* • Learn new words in combination with other words that often go with them	*Do we have enough for the party?* • Group work: Agree with group members on what to buy for a party
I hope you can come. • Listen to three people responding to different invitations, and complete a chart *What should I do with these?* • Listen to three people discuss unwanted items, and identify what they do with them	*Getting rid of clutter* • An article giving ideas on ways to manage clutter and offering solutions to readers' problems	• Write a question about a personal clutter problem, and write a reply to a classmate's question • Link ideas with *as long as, provided that,* and *unless*	*Do your best!* • Use a new expression in a sentence; then add another sentence to make its meaning clear	*Who's going to do what?* • Group work: Choose an event and prepare a list of all the things you need to get ready for it

Touchstone **checkpoint Units 4–6** **pages 63–64**

	Functions / Topics	Grammar	Vocabulary	Conversation strategies	Pronunciation
Unit 7 **Relationships** pages 65–74	- Talk about friendships - Discuss dating - Talk about relationships with neighbors	- Subject relative clauses - Object relative clauses - Phrasal verbs	- Phrasal verbs, including expressions to talk about relationships	- Soften comments with expressions like *I think, probably, kind of,* and *in a way* - Use *though* to give a contrasting idea	- Stress in phrasal verbs
Unit 8 **What if?** pages 75–84	- Talk about how you wish your life were different and why - Discuss how to deal with everyday dilemmas	- Use *wish* + past form of verb to talk about wishes for the present or future - Conditional sentences with *if* clauses about imaginary situations	- Expressions with verbs and prepositions	- Give advice using expressions like *If I were you . . . , I would . . . ,* and *You might want to . . .* - Use expressions with *That would be . . .* to comment on an idea or suggestion	- Intonation in long questions
Unit 9 **Tech savvy?** pages 85–94	- Discuss gadgets and technology - Ask for and offer help with technology problems	- Questions within sentences - Separable phrasal verbs with objects - *how to* + verb, *where to* + verb, and *what to* + verb	- Phrasal verbs, including expressions to talk about operating electronic machines and gadgets	- Give a different opinion - Use expressions like *You know what I mean?* to ask for agreement	- Link final consonants and initial vowels

Touchstone **checkpoint Units 7–9** **pages 95–96**

	Functions / Topics	Grammar	Vocabulary	Conversation strategies	Pronunciation
Unit 10 **What's up?** pages 97–106	- Discuss your social life - Talk about different kinds of movies - Recommend books, CDs, movies, and shows	- Present perfect continuous vs. present perfect - *Since, for,* and *in* for duration - *Already, still,* and *yet* with present perfect	- Kinds of movies - Expressions to describe types of movies	- Ask for a favor politely - Use *All right* and *OK* to move the conversation to a new phase or topic and to agree to requests	- Reduction of *have*
Unit 11 **Impressions** pages 107–116	- Speculate about people and situations - Talk about feelings and reactions	- Modal verbs *must, may, might, can't,* or *could* for speculating - Adjectives ending in *-ed* vs. adjectives ending in *-ing*	- Feelings and reactions	- Show you understand another person's feelings or situation - Use *You see* to explain a situation - Use *I see* to show you understand	- Linking and deletion with *must*
Unit 12 **In the news** pages 117–126	- Talk about events in the news - Talk about extreme weather and natural disasters	- The simple past passive - The simple past passive with *by* + agent - Adverbs with the passive	- Extreme weather conditions - Natural disasters	- Introduce news with expressions like *Did you hear (about) . . . ?, Guess what?,* and *You know what?* - Use the expression *The thing is . . .* to introduce issues	- Breaking sentences into parts

Touchstone **checkpoint Units 10–12** **pages 127–128**

Listening	Reading	Writing	Vocabulary notebook	Free talk
People I look forward to seeing ▪ Fill in the missing words describing three people; then listen for the reasons the speaker likes to see them *Getting back in touch* ▪ Identify the people the speaker wants to get back in touch with; then write the reason he lost touch with them	*Web site chaperones classmate reunions* ▪ A newspaper article about a Web site that reunites former classmates	▪ Write a short article about three friends and the things you have in common ▪ Use *both*, *both of us*, and *neither of us* to talk about things in common	*Matching up* ▪ Learn new phrasal verbs by writing other verbs that can go with the particle and other particles that can go with the same verb	*What's important?* ▪ Group work: Discuss and agree on the five most important things to consider when choosing a life partner
A wish for today ▪ Identify the topics as four people talk about their wishes; then write the reasons *Here's my advice.* ▪ Compare the advice that three people give; then decide whose advice is most helpful	*If I had my life to live over, . . .* ▪ An article listing ways the writer's life would be different if it could be lived over	▪ Write an article on the changes you would make if you could live last year over again ▪ Use adverbs of certainty in affirmative and negative statements	*Imagine that!* ▪ Learn prepositions that can follow a new verb	*What would you do?* ▪ Group work: Discuss the questions about hypothetical situations, and find out what you have in common
What do you know about the Internet? ▪ Answer the questions about the Internet, and then listen to a conversation to check answers; then write more information *The problem with technology* ▪ Listen to two people giving opinions, and identify each person's opinions; then agree or disagree with two opinions	*Robbing you blind?* ▪ A magazine article about identity theft and what can be done to avoid it	▪ Write a short article giving dos and don'ts for keeping personal information safe ▪ Plan your article	*On and off* ▪ Write short conversations about everyday situations to remember new vocabulary	*Tech trivia* ▪ Pair work: Ask and answer general technology questions, and figure out your partner's score

Touchstone **checkpoint Units 7–9   pages 95–96**

Listening	Reading	Writing	Vocabulary notebook	Free talk
A small favor ▪ Match four students with the favor each asks the professor; then decide if you agree with the professor's decision *I'd really recommend it.* ▪ Listen for details as two friends talk about a review of a show	*Home entertainment* ▪ A review of a movie and a CD	▪ Write a review of a book, CD, movie, or show ▪ Introduce contrasting ideas with *although*, *even though*, and *even if*	*Great movies* ▪ Link new words and expressions to things you have recently done or seen	*Who's been doing what?* ▪ Class activity: Ask your classmates questions about their recent activities
People and situations ▪ Match four people and their situations; then write a response with *must* to each *People making a difference* ▪ Match three people and the organizations they work with; then write what each organization does	*A teen hero* ▪ A magazine article describing an inspirational teen	▪ Write a letter to the editor ▪ Use expressions for giving impressions, reactions, and opinions	*How would you feel?* ▪ Link new words for feelings to the situations where you would experience those feelings	*What on earth are they doing?* ▪ Pair work: Look at two photos, and speculate about what is happening
News update ▪ Listen to two news stories, and answer questions *What do they say next?* ▪ Predict the topic of four conversations; match their beginnings and endings; then listen to check your answers	*A new brand of journalism is taking root in South Korea* ▪ A news article about a new way of reporting the news	▪ Write a report on class survey results about keeping up with the news ▪ Learn useful expressions for writing about statistics	*Forces of nature* ▪ Learn new words in combination with other words that are typically used with them	*Here's the news!* ▪ Pair work: Create short news reports about photos

Touchstone **checkpoint Units 10–12   pages 127–128**

Working in groups

Does anyone else have anything to add?

What do you think, _____ ?

Let's take turns asking the questions. . . .
OK, who wants to go first?

Do you want me to make the list?

Should I write down the information this time?

Do you have any ideas, _____ ?

Do you know what the answer is?

We're going to do a role play about _____ .

In our survey, we found out that _____ .

We agreed on these things. First, . . .

We're finished. What should we do next?

Checking your partner's work

Can you help me with this question? I'm stuck.

I can't figure out this answer. Can you help me?

Would you mind checking my work?

Let's compare answers.

Let's exchange papers.

I can't read your writing. What does this say?

I'm not sure what you mean.
Do you mean _____ ?

I don't understand what this means.
Are you trying to say _____ ?

Your blog was really interesting. I just wanted
to ask you a question about _____ .

I was wondering about _____ .

The way we are

In Unit 1, you learn how to . . .

- use manner adverbs and adjectives to talk about people's behavior and personality.
- use adverbs like *extremely* to make adjectives and adverbs stronger.
- add prefixes to adjectives to make opposites.
- use *always* with a continuous verb to describe individual habits.
- use *at least* to point out the positive side of a situation.

Before you begin . . .

Do you like people-watching? Look at the pictures.

- Who looks outgoing? shy? conservative? stylish?
- Which people would you like to meet? Why?

People in a hurry

Do you need to slow down?

Take this quiz to find out.

1 When I walk down the street, . . .

a I walk very fast and use the time to make phone calls.

b I enjoy the walk and look at the things and people around me.

2 When I go out to lunch with friends, . . .

a I eat quickly so that I can get back to my work.

b I eat slowly, and I enjoy the food and conversation.

3 When there's a family event, . . .

a I often have to miss it because I have too much to do.

b I try to plan my time well so that I can attend the event.

4 If traffic is heavy and some people are driving a bit recklessly, . . .

a I honk my horn a lot. I get mad easily in bad traffic.

b I automatically slow down and try to drive carefully.

5 If I'm waiting at the airport and find out that my flight is delayed, . . .

a I get impatient and complain to the people behind the counter.

b I wait patiently. I read something or make a few phone calls.

6 If I'm in a hurry and think people are talking too slowly, . . .

a I sometimes interrupt them to finish their sentences.

b I listen quietly and wait for them to finish before I talk.

7 If I play a game or sport with friends, . . .

a I take the game seriously, and I feel very bad if I lose.

b I think it's nicer to win than lose, but I don't feel strongly about it.

8 If I get an assignment with a very tight deadline, . . .

a I get very stressed – I hate it when I don't have time to do a job properly.

b I work hard to do the best I can in the time I have.

Mostly A answers?
It's time to slow down and enjoy life more. Try to plan your time differently. Make more time for family, friends, and fun.

Mostly B answers?
You're balancing work and play nicely. Just keep the balance right.

1 Getting started

A Listen and take the quiz. For each item, circle *a* or *b*.

About you → **B** *Pair work* Compare your quiz responses with a partner. How are you alike? different?

Figure it out → **C** Circle the correct words. Which sentences are true for you? Tell a partner.

1. I listen to people **careful / carefully**.
2. I'm a **quiet / quietly** person.
3. I get **impatient / impatiently** in long lines.
4. I take school and work very **serious / seriously**.

2

2 Grammar *Manner adverbs vs. adjectives*

Verb + manner adverb	**Adjective + noun**	**be, feel, get, etc. + adjective**
I wait **patiently** in lines.	I'm a **patient** person.	I'm **patient**.
He doesn't sing very **well**.	He's not a **good** singer.	His voice sounds **terrible**.
He drives very **fast**.	He's a **fast** driver.	He gets **reckless** sometimes.
She drives **carefully**.	She's a **careful** driver.	I feel **safe*** with her.
		***But:** I feel **strongly** about it.

Regular -ly adverbs	**Irregular adverbs**
patient → patient**ly**	good → **well**
careful → careful**ly**	late → **late**
easy → eas**ily**	fast → **fast**
automatic → automatic**ally**	hard → **hard**

▶ **In conversation . . .**

The most common **-ly** manner adverbs are **quickly**, **easily**, **differently**, **automatically**, **slowly**, **properly**, **badly**, **strongly**, and **carefully**.

A Complete these opinions about modern life. Use the correct form of the words.

1. Young people don't dress _____ (proper) these days. They don't wear _____ (appropriate) clothes.
2. Parents see things very _____ (different) from their children, so families argue a lot.
3. Young people don't know how to speak _____ (correct). They use a lot of slang.
4. Nobody feels _____ (safe) on the highways because people drive too _____ (fast) and _____ (reckless).
5. On buses, people seem very _____ (rude). They don't _____ (automatic) give their seats to older people.
6. People are getting very _____ (impatient). They expect you to answer their e-mails _____ (immediate).

> **About you**

B *Group work* Discuss the opinions. Are they true in your country or city?

"I think young people dress properly here. I mean, they often dress casually, but that's OK."

3 Speaking naturally *Questions giving alternatives*

Are you usually on time for class? Or do you often arrive late?

A Listen and repeat the questions above. Notice how the intonation rises in the first question and falls in the second question.

> **About you**

B Now listen and repeat these pairs of questions. Then ask and answer the questions with a partner.

1. Do you try hard to get to every class? Or do you sometimes skip classes?
2. Do you listen to the teacher carefully? Or do you often think about other things?
3. Do you do your homework properly? Or do you just do it quickly?
4. Do you learn new grammar easily? Or do you have to work hard at it?
5. Do you write down new words automatically? Or do you just try to remember them?

Personality and character

1 Building vocabulary and grammar

A Listen and read. Who do these people admire? Do you know any people with these qualities?

Who is someone you **really** admire?

"My English teacher. She's incredibly **talented** and **creative**. And she **has a great sense of humor**. She's pretty **disorganized**, though. She forgets something almost every class, but her classes are absolutely wonderful!"

Lisa Marks

"I really admire a guy in my karate class. He's extremely **competitive**, but when he wins, he's not **arrogant** like some of the other guys. He's not very **outgoing**, so some people think he's **unfriendly**, but I think he's basically just **shy**."

Peter Zukowski

Keith Lee

"I think my dad's a pretty cool guy. We get along really well. He's fairly **easygoing** and **laid-back**. And he's very **practical** and **down-to-earth**, so he always gives me good advice. Also, he's completely **honest** with me. I can trust what he says."

Eva Sanchez

"My friend Luisa. She's so **helpful** and **generous**. I mean, she's always doing things for other people. She's not **selfish** at all. And she's totally **reliable**. If she says she'll help you with something, she does. You can always count on her."

Word sort

B Which of the personality words or expressions above describe these qualities? Compare with a partner.

Winning is very important to you.	competitive	*People can always count on you.*	
You handle everyday problems well.		*You're overly proud of yourself.*	
You give a lot of time or money to people.		*You're not well organized.*	
You tell the truth, and never cheat or steal.		*You're relaxed about life.*	

Figure it out

C How many words can you find in the article that make adjectives stronger? Make a list. Then compare with a partner.

> incredibly

2 Grammar *Adverbs before adjectives and adverbs* 💿

Use *incredibly, extremely, very, really, so, pretty, and fairly* **to make some adjectives and adverbs stronger.**	She's **incredibly** talented. She's **extremely** generous. He's a **pretty** cool guy. We get along **really** well.	***Adjective prefixes*** patient → **im**patient considerate → **in**considerate friendly → **un**friendly reliable → **un**reliable honest → **dis**honest organized → **dis**organized
Use *absolutely* **or** *really* **(but not** *very***) with adjectives that are already very strong.**	She's **absolutely** wonderful. He's **really** fantastic.	
The expression *at all* **makes negatives stronger.**	She's **not** selfish **at all**.	
***Completely* and *totally* mean 100%.**	He's **completely** honest. She's **totally** reliable.	

▶ **In conversation . . .**

People use **really** and **pretty** much more often in conversation than in writing.

really 🗨🗨🗨🗨🗨🗨🗨🗨🗨 : ✏
pretty 🗨🗨🗨🗨🗨🗨🗨 : ✏

About you → Do you know people with these qualities? Write a sentence for each expression, and follow it with an example. Then compare sentences with a partner.

1. totally honest
2. fairly laid-back
3. not reliable at all
4. extremely talented
5. really competitive
6. completely disorganized
7. very impatient
8. incredibly generous
9. absolutely wonderful

"My mother is totally honest. She always tells the truth."

3 Listening and speaking *Best friends*

A 💿 Listen to the interviews. What do the three people say about their best friends? Complete the chart.

	Matt	Maria	Lucas
What's your best friend like?	He's a fun person.		
What do you have in common?			
How are you different?			

About you → **B** *Pair work* Ask and answer the questions with a partner.

A **What's your best friend like?**
B **She has a great sense of humor, and . . .**

4 Vocabulary notebook *Happy or sad?*

See page 10 for a new way to log and learn vocabulary.

He's always working.

1 Conversation strategy *Describing individual habits*

A Read the sentences. Who is describing a habit, Kate or Jenny?

Kate My brother is always borrowing my car, and it's so annoying.
Jenny Sometimes my brother borrows my car, but that's OK.

Now listen. What's Jacob's roommate like?

Alexis So, how's your new roommate working out?

Jacob Well, I don't see that much of him, really. I mean, he's always working, you know, at the library or sitting at the computer.

Alexis Well, at least he's not always throwing wild parties or playing music all night.

Jacob Yeah. And he's pretty easygoing. I'm always borrowing his stuff, and he doesn't mind.

Alexis He sounds better than my old roommate. She was so unpleasant.

Jacob You're right, she was pretty bad.

Alexis Yeah. She was always talking about people behind their backs.

Jacob You mean like we're doing right now?!

Notice how Alexis and Jacob use *always* and a continuous verb to talk about things people do a lot or more than is usual. Find other examples in the conversation.

"He's always working."

B Change the underlined parts of these sentences to describe habits. Use *always* and a continuous verb. Compare with a partner.

1. I'm pretty disorganized. I <u>lose</u> things. *I'm always losing things.*
2. Everyone in my family loves music. We <u>sing</u> together.
3. My brother is really generous with his time. He <u>fixes</u> my computer.
4. My father is a workaholic. He <u>comes</u> home late. And he <u>brings</u> work home with him, too.
5. My college roommate was really funny. She <u>made</u> us laugh. You know, she <u>told</u> jokes.
6. A friend of mine <u>complains</u> she's broke, but she <u>buys</u> herself expensive clothes.
7. One of my friends is totally unreliable. He <u>cancels</u> plans at the last minute.

About you → **C** *Pair work* Tell your partner about your habits or the habits of your family or friends. Use the ideas above or your own ideas.

"My brother's really funny. He's always telling jokes."

SELF-STUDY
AUDIO CD
CD-ROM

2 Strategy plus *at least*

You can use the expression **at least** to point out the positive side of a situation.

Well, at least he's not always throwing wild parties.

> **In conversation . . .**
>
> **At least** is one of the top 500 words and expressions.

Find two places to add *at least* in each conversation. Then practice with a partner.

1. A My girlfriend is always late for our dates, so she's always apologizing to me. It drives me crazy.

   B Yeah, but‸at least she apologizes. My girlfriend never says she's sorry when she's late.

   A I know, and my girlfriend calls to say she'll be late.

2. A My friend is always borrowing my CDs and then giving them back weeks later.

   B Well, he returns them to you.

   A Yeah, and he never damages any of them.

3. A My brother is always getting good grades. It's impossible to keep up with him.

   B Yeah, but you're doing your best, right?

   A That's true. And I enjoy my classes.

3 Talk about it *Funny little habits*

Group work In your group, who's always doing these things? Discuss the questions. Can you think of something positive to say about your habit?

Who is always . . .

- ► checking phone messages?
- ► eating candy or chewing gum?
- ► falling asleep in class?
- ► singing or whistling?
- ► forgetting things?

- ► telling jokes?
- ► losing things?
- ► daydreaming?
- ► breaking things?
- ► looking in mirrors?

A *So, who's always checking phone messages?*
B *Well, I'm always checking my messages, but at least I don't do it in class.*

7

1 Reading

A Do you know an interesting fact about a famous person? Tell the class.

B Read the biographies. Which fact do you think is most interesting about each person?

Five things you
didn't know about . . .

❶ Alicia Keys
Pianist and singer-songwriter

1. Alicia Keys was born and raised in New York City.

2. She started playing the piano at the age of five. Her mother was very supportive and always encouraged Alicia to continue playing.

3. She got excellent grades in high school and graduated at the age of 16.

4. A versatile performer, Alicia released her first CD when she was 19. She wrote one song on the CD when she was 14.

5. Her secret talent? She's good at swimming.

❸ Alex Rodriguez
Baseball player, New York Yankees

1. Alex Rodriguez was born in New York City, but he lived in the Dominican Republic for four years and learned to play baseball there.

2. He's a fantastic athlete but also very humble. Everyone agrees — he's a really nice guy!

3. He's generous with his time and money. He created an educational program called Grand Slam for Kids to help children improve their academic skills.

4. He loves to shop for nice clothes. Armani is his favorite designer.

5. He has impeccable grooming habits. He gets a haircut every ten days, and has a manicure and pedicure every month.

❷ Matt Damon
Actor and screenwriter

1. Actors can be demanding, but not Matt Damon. He's extremely polite and easygoing.

2. He's really smart. He studied English literature at Harvard University but left school to become an actor.

3. He writes well. He wrote the screenplay *Good Will Hunting* with his friend Ben Affleck, and they both starred in the film.

4. He (and Affleck) won an Academy Award for this screenplay.

5. He doesn't like to drive.

❹ Lucy Liu
Actor and artist

1. A native New Yorker, Lucy Liu has a degree in Asian languages and speaks Mandarin fluently.

2. She has studied art in China.

3. She's an accomplished artist. She has exhibited her photography and paintings in galleries in New York City and Los Angeles.

4. She's extremely athletic. She's good at horseback riding, rock climbing, and skiing.

5. She can play the accordion.

C *Pair work* Which person would you most like to meet? Why?

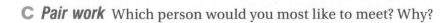

D Find the adjectives on the left in the biographies. Can you guess their meanings? Match the adjectives with the correct definitions on the right.

1. supportive _e_
2. versatile ___
3. demanding _d_
4. humble ___
5. impeccable ___
6. accomplished ___

a. multitalented, having many skills
b. modest, not talking too much about your abilities
c. talented, skillful
d. perfect
e. helpful and encouraging
f. difficult to please or work with

2 *Listening* *I didn't know that!*

A  Listen. What do these people say about themselves? Write the names in the chart.

Diana	Lincoln	Miguel	Natalie	Penny

Name	What the person says	Other information
Miguel	"I can speak Tagalog."	But I speak to languages < Spanish English
Natalie	"My first name is really Ashley."	
Penny	"I can be very impatient sometimes."	
Lincoln	"I really wanted to be a pilot."	
Diana	"I'm allergic to strawberries."	

B 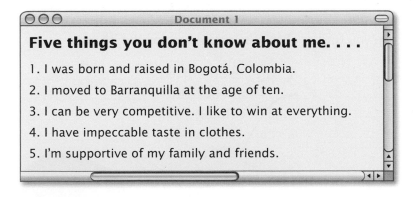 Listen again. What other information do you learn? Write one sentence about each person in the chart.

3 *Writing and speaking* *Your personal profile*

A What are five things people don't know about you? Write a profile, or short description, about yourself. Don't write your name on your profile.

```
○ ○ ○                Document 1

Five things you don't know about me. . . .

1. I was born and raised in Bogotá, Colombia.
2. I moved to Barranquilla at the age of ten.
3. I can be very competitive. I like to win at everything.
4. I have impeccable taste in clothes.
5. I'm supportive of my family and friends.
```

> **Help note**

Useful expressions

I was born and raised in . . .
At the age of 17, I . . .
I can be . . .
I work for a company **called** . . .
I'm an **accomplished** . . .
I started playing the flute . . .

B *Group work* Exchange profiles in your group. Take turns reading them aloud. Can your group guess who each one is about?

4 *Free talk* *People are interesting!*

See *Free talk 1* at the back of the book for more speaking practice.

Vocabulary notebook

Happy or sad?

Learning tip Learning opposite meanings

When you learn a new word, find out if it has an "opposite." Be careful – sometimes a word has different meanings and different opposites.

This exercise is hard.	→	This exercise is easy.
He's a hard worker.	→	He's lazy. He doesn't work hard.
This chair feels hard.	→	This chair feels soft.

People are positive!

Adjectives without prefixes are much more frequent in conversation.

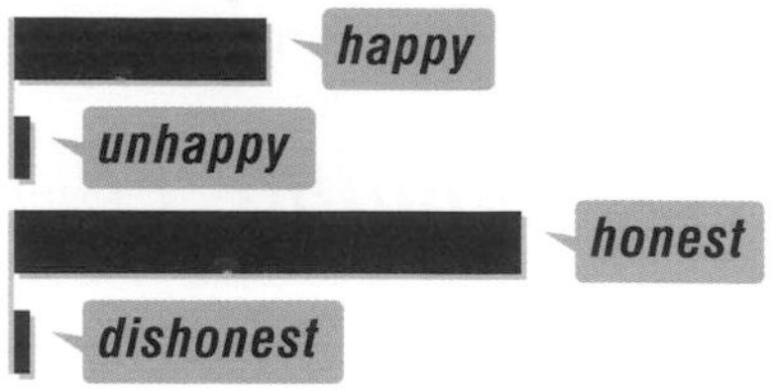

1 Rewrite the sentences so that they have an opposite meaning. Use the words in the box.

badly happy mean rude

1. My father drives really well. badly
2. My best friend can be very kind. rude
3. My boss is an extremely polite person. mean
4. I was pretty unhappy in school. happy

2 For each of the underlined words, think of a word with an opposite meaning.

1. I have a pretty loud voice. ______
2. My mother is extremely demanding. ______
3. I'm usually late for appointments. ______
4. My brother eats very quickly. ______
5. I think English is difficult. ______
6. My sister and I have similar tastes. ______

3 ***Word builder*** Use the prefixes *im-*, *in-*, *un-*, and *dis-* to create opposite meanings for these words. Use a dictionary to help you find or check the opposites you don't know.

1. He's **patient**. impatient
2. She's **honest**. ______
3. He's **friendly**. ______
4. He's **competent**. ______
5. They're **organized**. ______
6. He looks **healthy**. ______
7. She's **reliable**. ______
8. She's **considerate**. ______

On your own

Choose 3 photos of friends or family members. Write 5 things about each person's personality or character, and a sentence about something they typically do.

Experiences

In Unit 2, you learn how to . . .

- use the present perfect with regular and irregular verbs.
- ask and answer questions beginning with *Have you ever . . . ?*
- use the simple past to give specific answers to questions in the present perfect.
- talk about experiences you have or haven't had.
- keep a conversation going.
- use *Do you?*, *Did you?*, or *Have you?* to show interest.

Before you begin . . .

Think of some special experiences you hope to have in the future. Tell the class . . .

- something you'd like to do.
- a place you'd like to go someday.
- a person you'd like to meet.
- something you'd like to see.

We asked five people, "What's your secret dream?"

"Actually, I've always wanted to be an actor. I haven't had any formal training, but I've been in a couple of college plays. So my dream is to study acting."

– Jill Richardson
Vancouver, Canada

"Well, Carlos and I have gone sailing a few times with friends, and we've had a lot of fun. So our dream is to buy our own sailboat. But we haven't saved enough money!"

– Sonia and
Carlos Silva
Brasília, Brazil

"My dream? To go surfing. I've never tried it before, but my brother goes surfing all the time! He's even surfed in Hawai'i."

– Raquel Garza
Monterrey, Mexico

"Well, my parents have never traveled outside of Japan, so I want to take them to Europe. I've been there many times, so I know all the best places to go!"

– Hiro Tanaka
Osaka, Japan

1 Getting started

A 💿 Listen. What is each person's secret dream? Do you have any secret dreams like these?

> **Figure it out** →

B Can you complete these sentences about the people above?

1. Jill Richardson has always _____ to be an actor.
2. Sonia and Carlos Silva _____ saved enough money to buy a sailboat.
3. Raquel Garza _____ never tried surfing before.
4. Hiro Tanaka's parents _____ never been to Europe.

12

2 Grammar *Present perfect statements* 💿

Use the present perfect for events at an indefinite time before now.

I	**'ve been** to Europe.		I	**haven't been** to Paris.
You	**'ve done** a lot of things.		You	**haven't gone** sailing.
We	**'ve had** a lot of fun.		We	**haven't saved** enough money.
They	**'ve traveled** in Asia.		They	**haven't been** to Europe.
He	**'s surfed** in Hawai'i.		She	**hasn't tried** surfing before.

Regular past participles

travel	traveled	**traveled**
want	wanted	**wanted**
save	saved	**saved**
try	tried	**tried**

The present perfect is often used with these frequency expressions.

I've **always** wanted to study acting.
We've gone sailing **once / twice / many times**.
She's **never** tried it **before**.

Irregular past participles

be	was / were	**been**
do	did	**done**
go	went	**gone**
have	had	**had**
see	saw	**seen**

▶ *In conversation . . .*

When people talk about travel destinations, they generally use ***been*** as an alternative to ***gone*** to mean "gone somewhere and come back," as in *I've (never)* ***been*** *to Paris*. People use ***went*** (not ***was / were***) in past tense sentences, as in *I* ***went*** *to Paris last year*.

A Complete the conversations with the present perfect. Then practice with a partner.

1. *A* I _____ always _____ (want) to try scuba diving.
   B Really? Not me. I _____ always _____ (be) afraid of deep water.

2. *A* I _____ (not do) anything fun lately.
   B Me neither. I _____ (not have) any time.

3. *A* I _____ (not see) the new *Spider-Man* movie. I really want to see it.
   B We should go! All my friends _____ (see) it, and they loved it.

4. *A* I _____ (go) windsurfing three or four times this year. It's fun.
   B Can I go with you sometime? I _____ never _____ (try) it before.

5. *A* I want to go to Europe. I _____ never _____ (be) to Paris.
   B Me neither. My cousin lives there. He _____ (invite) me several times, but I _____ (not have) enough money to go.

> About you

B *Pair work* Start the conversations like the ones above. Change the underlined words.

"I've always wanted to try hang gliding."   *"Really? Not me. I've always been afraid of flying."*

3 Talk about it *What are your secret dreams?*

Group work Discuss the questions. Do you share any of the same dreams?

► What's something you've always wanted to buy?
► What's a city that you've never been to but would like to visit?
► What's something you've always wanted to learn how to do?
► What's something else you've always wanted to do?

13

1 Building language

A  Listen. Which experience do you think was scarier?

Have you ever done anything scary?

"Yes, I have. I went white-water rafting in Ecuador last year, and I fell off the raft. Luckily, my friends pulled me out of the river. But I've never been so scared in my life."

– Mei-ling Chen
Taipei, Taiwan

"No, I haven't. Well, maybe once. I entered a talent contest a couple of years ago and sang in front of a hundred people. That was scary. But I won third place!"

– Martín Suárez
Caracas, Venezuela

Figure it out

B Pair work Can you complete these questions and answers? Then practice with a partner.

1. *A* _____ you ever been to Ecuador?
   B Yes, I have. I _____ there last year.

2. *A* Have you ever _____ a talent contest?
   B No, I _____ . I've always _____ too shy.

2 Grammar Present perfect and simple past questions and answers

Use the present perfect for indefinite times before now.	**Have** you ever **gone** white-water rafting? No, I **haven't**. **I've** never **gone** rafting. Yes, I **have**. I **went** rafting last May.
Use the simple past for specific events or times in the past.	**Did** you **have** a good time? Yes, I **did**. But I **fell** off the raft.

▶ **In conversation . . .**

The most common questions with the present perfect are *Have you (ever) seen / been / heard / had . . . ?*

A Complete the conversations with the present perfect or simple past. Then practice with a partner.

1. *A* _____ your family _____ (have) a vacation last year?
   B Yes, we _____ . We _____ (go) to Bangkok in May.

2. *A* _____ you ever _____ (see) the Pyramids?
   B No, I _____ . I _____ always _____ (want) to go to Egypt.

3. *A* _____ you _____ (go) away last weekend?
   B No, we _____ . We _____ (stay) home.

4. *A* _____ you ever _____ (go) skiing?
   B Yes, I _____ . Actually, I _____ (go) many times. Last year, I _____ (ski) in the Andes.

The Royal Pantheon at the Grand Palace, Bangkok, Thailand

About you

B Pair work Ask the questions above. Answer with your own information.

3 Building vocabulary

A Ask your classmates about these good and bad experiences. For each question, find someone who answers yes. Write the student's name in the chart.

Good experiences		Bad experiences	
Have you ever . . .	**Name**	**Have you ever . . .**	**Name**
won a contest or competition?		**broken** something valuable?	
gotten a perfect grade on an exam?		**lost** something important?	
spoken to a famous person?		**had** the flu?	
taken an exciting trip?		**forgotten** an important appointment?	
found a lot of money?		**fallen** and **hurt** yourself?	

"Have you ever won a contest?"   *"Yes, I have. I won a spelling contest in eighth grade."*

B Complete the verb chart. Add more verbs that you know.

Base form	win			find			fall	
Simple past	won	got	took		lost		forgot	hurt
Past participle	won	spoken				had		

4 Speaking naturally *Reduced and unreduced forms of have*

A **Have** you ever been to Mexico?
B No, I **have**n't. But my parents **have** been there several times.   (parents**'ve**)

A Listen and repeat the question and answer above. Notice how *have* is reduced in questions and full statements but not in short answers.

About you **B** *Group work* Complete the questions with ideas from the group. Then ask and answer your questions. If you answer yes, give a specific example.

1. Have you ever tried _____ ?
2. Have you ever been to _____ ?
3. Have you ever seen _____ ?
4. Have you ever taken a _____ class?
5. Have you ever had _____ food?
6. Have you ever lost _____ ?

A *Have you ever tried parasailing?*
B *Actually, I have. I went parasailing last summer. It was really fun.*
C *No, I haven't. But I'd like to.*

5 Vocabulary notebook *Have you ever . . . ?*

See page 20 for a useful way to log and learn vocabulary.

Lesson C — I've heard it's good.

Conversation strategy *Keeping the conversation going*

A How can you show interest and keep this conversation going? Choose the best answer.

A Have you seen the new Nicole Kidman movie?

B ☐ No, I haven't.

☐ No, but I've heard about it. Have you seen it?

☐ No, I don't like comedies.

Now listen. What do Hal and Debra have in common?

Debra Have you seen any good movies lately?

Hal Well, I just saw that new Jim Carrey movie. Have you seen it?

Debra No, but I've heard it's good. Did you like it?

Hal Yeah, it was incredibly funny. Do you like comedies?

Debra Yeah. I have to go see it. I love Jim Carrey.

Hal Do you? Uh, are you a Will Smith fan?

Debra Umm . . . I've heard of him. Is he good?

Hal Yeah, I've seen most of his movies.

Debra Have you? Oh, look, here's a Will Smith film.

Hal Oh, I haven't seen that one. Do you want to go?

Debra Yeah. I'm kind of in the mood for a comedy.

Notice how Debra and Hal keep the conversation going. They say things like *I've heard it's good* to show interest and then ask a question. Find other examples in the conversation.

> "Have you seen it?"
> "No, but I've heard it's good. Did you like it?"

B Match each statement with a response. Then practice with a partner.

1. My favorite movie is *Spirited Away.* Have you ever seen it? _____
2. Have you ever eaten a <u>durian</u>? _____
3. Do you know that new band called <u>Sunset</u>? They're really great. _____
4. One of my favorite restaurants is <u>Silk Road</u>. Have you ever eaten there? _____

a. It's a fruit, right? I've never tried it. What does it taste like?
b. No, but I've walked by it. What kind of food do they serve?
c. No, but I've heard good things about them. Do you have any of their CDs?
d. I've heard of it. What's it about?

About you → **C** *Pair work* Practice the conversations above using your own ideas. Change the underlined words.

SELF-STUDY AUDIO CD CD-ROM

2 *Strategy plus* *Response questions*

You can show interest by responding with short questions like *Do you?* and *Have you?* Use the same tense as the other person.

> I love Jim Carrey.

> Do you?

Complete the conversations with response questions like *Do you?*, *Are you?*, *Did you?*, or *Have you?* Then practice with a partner.

In conversation . . .

To show surprise, you can respond with questions like **You do?** and **You have?** This is more informal.

1. *A* Have you ever gone up in a hot-air balloon?
    B No. I'm scared of heights.
    A _____ ? Me too. And I get sick on airplanes, too.
    B _____ ? I'm the same way. I hate flying.

2. *A* Have you ever performed in front of an audience?
    B Yes, I have. Actually, I do it all the time.
    A _____ ? Wow.
    B Yeah. I'm a drummer in a jazz band.
    A _____ ? I'm impressed!

3. *A* Have you been to any good restaurants lately?
    B Well, I tried that new Turkish restaurant last week.
    A _____ ? I've been there a couple of times, too.
    B _____ ? Did you like it?

3 *Listening* *What have they done?*

A 🔵 Listen. What is each person talking about? Check (✓) the topic.

❶ *Philip*
☐ famous people
☐ photography
☐ a vacation in Greece

❷ *Sarah*
☐ a sports injury
☐ a competition
☐ an old friend

❸ *Melissa*
☐ a science exam
☐ an accident
☐ a math class

B 🔵 Listen again. Respond with surprise to the last thing each person says. Check (✓) the boxes.

	You have?	You do?	You did?
1. Philip	☐	☐	☐
2. Sarah	☐	☐	☐
3. Melissa	☐	☐	☐

4 *Free talk* *Can you believe it? I've never done that!*

See *Free talk 2* at the back of the book for more speaking practice.

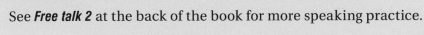

1 Reading

A Do you ever read "blogs," or Web logs, on the Internet? Are you a "blogger"? Do you know anyone who writes an online journal? Tell the class.

B Read the two blogs. Which blogger's experiences are the most interesting to you? Why?

Joshua's Blog

Greetings from the Galápagos

Puerto Ayora, Ecuador (Galápagos Islands)
Saturday, November 20, 2004

All is well in Puerto Ayora. I have been very busy. In the last three weeks, I have snorkeled and been scuba diving with giant green turtles, sea lions, penguins, and numerous species of tropical fish. I've wandered over fields of black volcanic rocks, through rocky beaches teeming with fat, lazy iguanas and red, yellow, and blue crabs. I've seen giant Galápagos tortoises and all sorts of rare birds.

I'm flying back to Quito on Tuesday. After that, I plan to go to Peru.

Posted by Joshua on November 20, 2004, 08:28 p.m.

Source: *BootsnAll Travel Network*

Suzanne's Blog

I'M IN ATHENS!

Thursday, June 10, 2004
Well, after 24 hours of travel, I have landed in Greece! Athens is beautiful! The most incredible experience I've had today is figuring out that I can read! I have spent all of about two hours over the past month studying the Greek alphabet, but I was amazed to find out once I got here that I can actually read Greek! I didn't realize how quickly I was learning the Greek alphabet. My cab driver probably thought I was crazy because I was reading every sign and asking him if I was right.

Thursday, June 17, 2004
As for the island of Lesvos, well, it's perfect . . . absolutely perfect. I have been all around the world, and I think that it is the most beautiful place I have ever been. The sea is so crystal clear that you can see your shadow in water 10 meters deep. The beaches are incredible, and there are these amazing little towns nestled in the mountains — every one like it's straight off a postcard.

Posted by Suzanne on June 10 and June 17, 2004.

Source: *Suzanne Moyer's Little Corner of the World*

C *Pair work* Read the blogs again. Can you find . . .

1. three things Joshua did on his trip?
2. six kinds of wildlife Joshua saw?
3. the reason why Suzanne was pleased with herself in Athens?
4. three reasons why Suzanne thought Lesvos was absolutely perfect?

2 Listening A traveler's adventures

A 🔘 Listen to Kevin talk about an e-mail he received from his friend Pamela. Check (✓) the things Pamela has done.

❶ ☐   ❷ ☐   ❸ ☐   ❹ ☐   ❺ ☐

B 🔘 Listen again. Answer the questions.

1. Where is Pamela? _____

2. Why is she there? _____

3. What's the weather like? _____

4. What did Pamela want to try? _____

5. Why hasn't she been able to do it? _____

3 Writing and speaking A blog

A Think about an exciting experience you've had, and write a blog about it. Do you have a photo to add to the blog?

○ ○ ○   Document 1

Flying above the rain forest

Last summer, I went on the Sky Trek in the rain forest in Monteverde, Costa Rica. I'm afraid of heights, so I almost didn't go. Fortunately, there were some great guides, and they really helped me. Amazingly, it wasn't really scary. It was the most exciting experience I've ever had! I didn't see a quetzal bird, unfortunately, so maybe I'll go back.

> **Help note**
>
> ### Adverbs of attitude
>
> Use adverbs like **fortunately**, **unfortunately**, **amazingly**, etc., to show your attitude or feeling about something.
>
> > **Fortunately**, there were some great guides.
> > **Amazingly**, it wasn't really scary.
> > I didn't see a quetzal bird, **unfortunately**.

B *Class activity* Take turns reading your classmates' blogs. Discuss who has . . .

- had the most exciting experience.
- done something you'd love to do.
- been somewhere you'd love to go.

Learning tip *Verb charts*

When you learn a new verb, write the three main forms in a chart.

base form	simple past	past participle
go	went	gone

Word builder Complete the charts. Do you know the past participles for all the verbs?

These verbs have three different forms.

be	was / were	been	drive	drove		break		broken
do	did		write		written	choose	chose	
go		gone	eat	ate		speak		spoken
see	saw		give		given	wake	woke	
drink		drunk	fall	fell		get		gotten
sing	sang		take		taken	forget	forgot	

For these verbs, the simple past form is the same as the past participle.

find	found	found	meet			win		
have			read			bring		
hear			say			buy		
keep			sell			catch		
leave			sit			teach		
make			tell			think		

For these verbs, the base form is the same as the past participle.

become	became	become
come		
run		

All forms of these verbs are the same.

cut	cut	cut
hurt		
put		

On your own

Make a "sentence string." Complete the sentence *I've never . . . .* How many different ideas can you think of?

I've never flown a plane, danced in the rain, . . .

Wonders of the world

In Unit 3, you learn how to . . .

- use the superlative form of adjectives.
- use the superlative with nouns.
- ask and answer questions about measurements with *How* + adjective . . . ?
- talk about human and natural wonders.
- use short responses to show you are a supportive listener.
- use superlatives for emphasis.

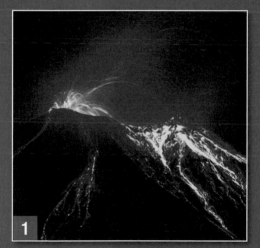

1
Arenal Volcano in Costa Rica has been continuously active since 1968.

2
This roller coaster at Thorpe Park in Great Britain turns riders upside down ten times.

3
The Great Canyon of Yarlung Tsangpo in Tibet is deeper than the Grand Canyon in the United States.

4
The Great Pyramid of Giza in Egypt dates from around 2560 BCE.

Before you begin . . .

Have you ever done any of these things?
Which would you really like to do?

- See an active volcano.
- Ride a scary roller coaster.
- Go hiking in a beautiful canyon.
- Visit an ancient city or monument.

Lesson A Human wonders

Test your knowledge. Can you guess the answers to these questions?

1. Which city has the tallest office building in the world?
a. Kuala Lumpur.   b. Taipei.   c. Chicago.

This building is 509 meters (1,670 feet) tall.

2. Where is the longest suspension bridge?
a. Japan.   b. Denmark.   c. China.

This is the longest suspension bridge in the world. It's 1,990 meters (6,529 feet) long.

3. Where is the largest shopping mall?
a. Canada.   b. Singapore.   c. The United States.

This mall has more than 800 stores and services, including 26 movie theaters.

4. Where is the busiest restaurant?
a. Seoul.   b. Bangkok.   c. Hong Kong.

This restaurant employs 1,000 workers and has 5,000 seats.

5. Which city has the biggest soccer stadium?
a. Rio de Janeiro.   b. Rome.   c. Tokyo.

This stadium has the most seats. It can hold over 200,000 people.

6. Which country is the most popular with tourists?
a. The United States.   b. Spain.   c. France.

About 75 million tourists visit this country every year.

1 Getting started

A Listen to the quiz. Can you guess the correct answers? Circle *a*, *b*, or *c*.
Compare with a partner. Check your answers on the last page of your book.

Figure it out

B Pair work Can you complete these questions? Then ask and answer with a partner.
Can you guess the correct answers? Check your answers on the last page of your book.

1. What's the _____ (big) train station in the world?
2. What's the _____ (busy) airport in the world?
3. What's the _____ (expensive) city in the world?

2 Grammar Superlatives

For short adjectives: *the* + **adjective** + *-est*	What's **the tallest** building in the world? What's **the busiest** restaurant?
For long adjectives: *the* + *most / least* + **adjective**	What's **the most interesting** city in your country? What's **the least expensive** store?
Irregular superlatives: *good* → *the best; bad* → *the worst*	What's **the best** country to visit? What's **the worst** problem in your country?
Superlatives with nouns: *the most* + **noun**	Which country has **the most tourism**? Which stadium has **the most seats**?

▶ **In conversation . . .**

The + *most* + **adjective** is about 20 times more common than *the* + *least* + **adjective**.

A Complete these questions about your country. Use the superlative form of the adjectives or the superlative with nouns.

1. What's _____ (large) city?
2. Which airport has _____ (flights) every day?
3. What's _____ (fast) way to travel?
4. What's _____ (beautiful) region?
5. Which city has _____ (tourism)?
6. What's _____ (famous) monument?
7. What's _____ (good) university?
8. What's _____ (bad) problem for people?

B *Pair work* Ask and answer the questions. Do you and your partner agree?

3 Speaking naturally Linking and deletion with superlatives

Link the final st to vowel sounds and the sounds /h, l, r, w, y/.	**Delete the final t, and link the s to most consonant sounds.**
What's the mo<u>st i</u>nteresting neighborhood?	*What area has the mo<u>s(t) t</u>raffic?*
What's the talle<u>st o</u>ffice building?	*What's the busie<u>s(t) m</u>all or shopping area?*
What's the bigge<u>st h</u>otel?	*Where's the bigge<u>s(t) s</u>tadium?*
What's the large<u>st l</u>ibrary?	*What's the be<u>s(t) s</u>ports team?*
What's the nice<u>st r</u>estaurant?	*What neighborhood has the mo<u>s(t) c</u>lubs?*
What's the faste<u>st w</u>ay to travel around?	*What's the mo<u>s(t) p</u>opular dance club?*
What's the olde<u>st u</u>niversity?	*What's the be<u>s(t) m</u>ovie theater?*

A Listen and repeat the questions above. Notice how the final *st* is linked to vowel sounds and the sounds /h, l, r, w, y/. However, the final *t* is deleted before – and the *s* is linked to – most consonant sounds.

B *Group work* Ask and answer the questions above about your city. Agree on an answer for each question. Tell the class.

Natural wonders

1 Building vocabulary and grammar

A Read the Web page. Which facts did you know? Which didn't you know?

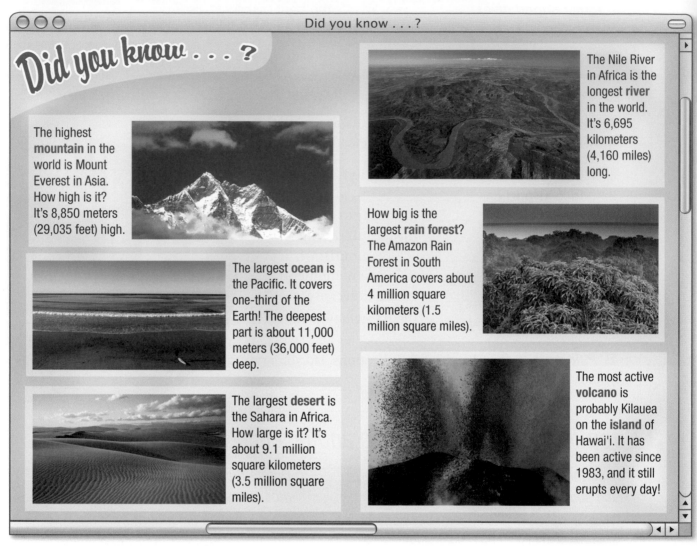

Did you know . . . ?

The highest **mountain** in the world is Mount Everest in Asia. How high is it? It's 8,850 meters (29,035 feet) high.

The largest **ocean** is the Pacific. It covers one-third of the Earth! The deepest part is about 11,000 meters (36,000 feet) deep.

The largest **desert** is the Sahara in Africa. How large is it? It's about 9.1 million square kilometers (3.5 million square miles).

The Nile River in Africa is the longest **river** in the world. It's 6,695 kilometers (4,160 miles) long.

How big is the largest **rain forest**? The Amazon Rain Forest in South America covers about 4 million square kilometers (1.5 million square miles).

The most active **volcano** is probably Kilauea on the **island** of Hawai'i. It has been active since 1983, and it still erupts every day!

Word sort ▸ **B** What natural features are in your country? Complete the chart with words from the Web page. Add other ideas. Then compare with a partner.

Features we have		Features we don't have	
beaches		desert	

"We have a lot of beaches."   *"The most beautiful beach is . . ."*   *"There are no deserts."*

Figure it out ▸ **C** Can you complete the question and answer?

How _____ is the Nile River?   It's 6,695 kilometers _____ .

2 Grammar Questions with How + adjective . . . ?

How high is Mount Everest?	It's 8,850 meters (29,035 feet) **high**.
How long is the Nile River?	It's 6,695 kilometers (4,160 miles) **long**.
How wide is the Grand Canyon?	It's about 29 kilometers (18 miles) **wide**.
How deep is the Pacific Ocean?	It's about 11,000 meters (36,000 feet) **deep**.
How large is the Sahara Desert?	It's 9.1 million square kilometers (3.5 million square miles).
How hot does it get in Death Valley?	It can reach 48 degrees Celsius (120 degrees Fahrenheit).

Some measurements can be followed by an adjective: *high, tall, long, wide, deep*

A Write two questions about each of these places.

1. the smallest continent / Australia / almost 7.7 million square kilometers
2. the highest mountain in South America / Mount Aconcagua / 6,962 meters
3. the longest river in Canada / the Mackenzie River / 4,241 kilometers
4. the widest canyon in the world / the Grand Canyon / 29 kilometers
5. the deepest lake in the world / Lake Baikal / 1,741 meters

> What's the smallest continent? How big is it?

AUSTRALIA

B *Pair work* Ask and answer your questions.

A ***What's the smallest continent?***	A ***How big is it?***
B ***Australia.***	B ***It's almost 7.7 million square kilometers.***

3 Listening What do you know?

A Take the quiz below. Then listen to the quiz show, and check your answers.

1. The world's tallest trees grow in _____ .
   a. Japan
   b. Brazil
   c. the United States

2. _____ is the highest lake in the world.
   a. Lake Victoria
   b. Lake Titicaca
   c. Lake Superior

3. The longest mountain range is _____ .
   a. the Andes
   b. the Himalayas
   c. the Rocky Mountains

4. The world's largest archipelago is _____ .
   a. the Philippines
   b. Greece
   c. Indonesia

B Listen again. Complete the sentences.

1. How tall are the world's tallest trees? They're _____ .
2. How high is the highest lake? It's _____ .
3. How long is the longest mountain range? It's _____ .
4. How many islands does the world's largest archipelago have? It has _____ .

4 Vocabulary notebook From the mountains to the sea

See page 30 for a useful way to log and learn vocabulary.

Conversation strategy *Being a supportive listener*

A What's the best way to agree with this statement?

A *This is the most beautiful beach!*

B _____

   a. Well, it's OK.   *b. Uh-huh.*   *c. Yeah, it really is.*

Now listen to Kim and Juan. What do they say about Sequoia National Park?

Kim	**This is the most incredible place!**
Juan	**Yeah, it really is. It feels good to be out of the city.**
Kim	**It sure does. You know, these trees are just awesome.**
Juan	**They really are. Have you ever been to Sequoia National Park?**
Kim	**No. Have you?**
Juan	**Yeah. I went last year. The trees there are the tallest in the world.**
Kim	**Really? I didn't know that.**
Juan	**Yeah. I had the best time. I mean, it's just the greatest place to hike.**
Kim	**We should go hiking there sometime.**
Juan	**You're right. We really should.**

Notice how Kim and Juan use short responses with *really* and *sure* to agree and to be supportive listeners. Find examples in the conversation.

"It feels good to be out of the city."
"It sure does."

B Match the comments on the left with the responses on the right. Then practice with a partner.

1. The weather was really <u>great</u> last Saturday. _____
2. This city doesn't have many <u>parks</u>. _____
3. We should <u>go snorkeling</u> sometime. _____
4. <u>Green Lake</u> is a great place to go swimming. _____
5. We've <u>had a lot of fun</u> today. _____

a. You're right. We really should.
b. Yeah, we sure have.
c. It sure is.
d. It really was. I spent the whole day outdoors.
e. No, it sure doesn't. That's too bad.

About you → **C Pair work** Practice the comments and responses using your own ideas. Change the underlined words.

SELF-STUDY AUDIO CD CD-ROM

26

2 Strategy plus *Using superlatives for emphasis*

You can use superlatives to emphasize your opinions or feelings.

This is the most incredible place!

I had the best time.

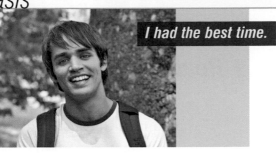

About you

Pair work Complete the answers with the superlative form of the adjectives. Then practice with a partner. Practice again with your own information.

1. *A* Should I stop in New York City when I go to the United States?
   B Well, I really liked it. You see _____ (interesting) people everywhere.

2. *A* How was your vacation? Was it fun?
   B Yeah. I went hiking in Peru, in the mountains. I had _____ (good) time.

3. *A* Have you ever been to the Galápagos Islands?
   B No, but I've read a lot about them. They have _____ (great) wildlife there.

4. *A* Have you ever heard of Angkor Wat in Cambodia?
   B Yeah. I've been there. It's _____ (amazing) place.

3 Listening and speaking *Travel talk*

A Listen to an interview on a radio show. In what order does Jill Ryan talk about these experiences? Number the photos.

☐ a Caribbean cruise

☐ a visit to Petra, Jordan

☐ a trip to Antarctica

☐ a train ride through the Copper Canyon in Mexico

B Listen again. How does Jill answer these questions? Complete the sentences.

1. What's the most interesting place you've ever been to?   Petra. It's _____ .
2. What's the most beautiful place you've seen?   Antarctica has _____ .
3. What's the best vacation you've had?   The Copper Canyon. The colors _____ .
4. What's the most exciting thing you've done on a trip?   I rode _____ .
5. What was your worst vacation?   The cruise was great, but I _____ .

About you

C Group work Discuss the questions. What experiences have people in your group had?

4 Free talk *The five greatest wonders*

See *Free talk 3* for more speaking practice.

1 Reading

A Read the headings of the paragraphs below on world records. Which three facts do you want to read about first? Tell the class.

B Read the facts. Do you know any facts like these about your country?

WORLD RECORDS

The fastest roller coaster . . .
The fastest roller coaster is Kingda Ka at Six Flags Great Adventure in New Jersey, U.S.A. It reaches a speed of 206 kilometers (128 miles) per hour in just four seconds! At 139 meters (456 feet), it's also the tallest roller coaster in the world.

The busiest subway . . .
The Metropolitan in Moscow, Russia, is the busiest subway system. More than 3 billion passengers ride on Moscow's Metro subways each year. It might also be the most beautiful subway system – many of the 150 stations have stained glass, marble statues, and chandeliers.

The most talkative bird . . .
The most proficient talking bird was an African gray parrot named Prudle. It learned over 800 words and could even conduct polite conversation.

The highest mountain range . . .
The world's highest mountain range is the Himalayas. It has 96 of the world's 109 peaks over 7,317 meters (24,000 feet).

The longest escalator . . .
The Central-Mid-Levels Escalator in Hong Kong, China, is the longest escalator in the world. It is 800 meters (2,625 feet) long and climbs 135 meters (443 feet).

The most expensive city . . .
According to the Mercer Human Resource Cost-of-Living Survey, the most expensive city is Tokyo, Japan. The survey compared the cost of goods and services in 144 cities.

The most visited city . . .
Tijuana, Mexico, located on the border with California, U.S.A., is the city with the most visitors. It has about 35 million tourists each year.

The highest city . . .
Wenchuan, China, at an altitude of 5,103 meters (16,730 feet) above sea level, is the world's highest city.

The deadliest animals . . .
The most poisonous amphibian is the poison dart frog, found in Central and South America. The poison in its skin can kill 20 adult humans.

The most poisonous snake is the African black mamba. The poison in one bite can kill 200 humans.

Sources: *Guinness World Records 2002, 2005; Scholastic Book of World Records 2005; www.edmunds.com; themeparks.about.com*

C *Pair work* Can you find this information in the paragraphs on page 28?

1. two very dangerous animals
2. two places at high altitudes
3. two different ways to go up nearly 140 meters (459 feet)
4. two places with crowds of people

2 *Speaking and writing* Interesting facts

A *Group work* Discuss these questions about your country. Find out as many facts as you can about each thing. Take notes.

What is . . .
- the highest mountain? the longest river?
- the longest bridge? the tallest building?
- the best-known natural feature?
- the best time of year to visit?
- the city with the most historic sites?

B Write a paragraph about a human or natural wonder in your country. Include a photo if you can.

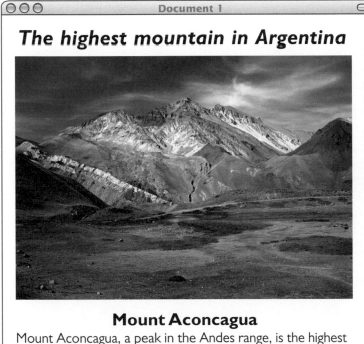

Document 1

The highest mountain in Argentina

Mount Aconcagua

Mount Aconcagua, a peak in the Andes range, is the highest mountain in Argentina. At 6,962 meters, it is the highest mountain in North and South America. Many people come to Argentina every year to climb Mount Aconcagua and to see the Andes, the longest mountain range in the world.

> **Help note**
>
> *Adding information*
>
> Mount Aconcagua is the highest mountain in Argentina. + It is a peak in the Andes range. =
>
> Mount Aconcagua, **a peak in the Andes range,** is the highest mountain in Argentina.
>
> Many people come to Argentina to see the Andes. + They are the longest mountain range in the world. =
>
> Many people come to Argentina to see the Andes, **the longest mountain range in the world.**

C *Group work* Take turns reading your paragraphs aloud. Did you learn any new information? Do you have any suggestions for additions or changes?

From the mountains to the sea

Learning tip *Drawing maps*

Draw a map of your country. Include natural features and important buildings or structures. Label your map.

We love water!

The 6 natural features people talk about most are:
1. lakes   3. mountains   5. oceans
2. beaches   4. rivers   6. valleys

1   Fill in the missing labels on this map of Australia.

- ✓ bridge
- desert
- island
- lake
- mountains
- ocean
- river

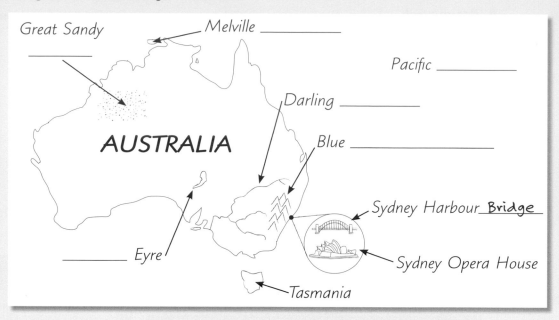

2   **Word builder**   Sketch a map of your country. Draw and label natural features and important buildings or monuments. Are any of these features in your country?

bay   **cliffs**   **coral reef**   **glacier**   **jungle**   **peninsula**   **valley**   **waterfall**

On your own

Find out the highest, longest, biggest, deepest, and largest natural features in your country. Label them on a map.

1 How much do you know about your partner?

A Complete the sentences with an adverb or adjective. Then make guesses about your partner by circling the affirmative or negative form of the verb.

Your guesses My partner . . .	Are your guesses . . .	
	right?	wrong?
1. (eats) / doesn't eat __slowly__ (slow).	☐	☐
2. listens / doesn't listen _____ (careful) to the weather forecast.	☐	☐
3. can draw / can't draw really _____ (good).	☐	☐
4. gets / doesn't get upset _____ (easy).	☐	☐
5. feels / doesn't feel _____ (bad) if he / she can't do a job _____ (proper).	☐	☐
6. tries / doesn't try _____ (hard) to be on time for appointments.	☐	☐

B *Pair work* Ask and answer questions to check your guesses. Show interest in what your partner says.

A *I guessed that you eat slowly. Do you?*
B *Actually, I do. I'm always the last person to finish a meal.*
A *You are? Well, it's probably a good idea to eat slowly.*

2 Have you ever?

Pair work Find out if your partner has ever done any of these things. Ask and answer questions. Give more information in your "yes" answers.

see someone famous	eat something unusual	win a prize or a competition	be late for an important event	break a bone
get sick and miss a class	have an argument	lose something important	buy yourself something special	throw a party

A *Have you ever seen someone famous?*
B *Yes, I have. I saw Jennifer Lopez last July.*
A *You did? That's amazing! Where did you see her?*

3 What natural and human wonders would you like to see?

Complete the chart with four natural and four human wonders. Then discuss with a partner.

Natural features		Buildings and structures	
volcano – Mt. Fuji			

"I'd really like to see Mt. Fuji. I've never seen it before. Have you seen it?"

31

4 Can you complete this conversation?

Complete the conversation with the words and expressions in the box. Use capital letters where necessary. Then practice with a partner.

I've ever seen	we really should	have you	at least	incredibly
✓I've heard	we sure did	I saw	always	the coolest

Sergio Have you been to the new sports complex?

Peter No, but _____I've heard_____ it's fabulous. How about you?

Sergio Actually, I've been there every weekend this summer.

Peter _____ ? What's it like?

Sergio Great. You see _____ people there. _____ Jillian and Maggie there Saturday. They're _____ hanging out at the skating rink.

Peter Maybe we should go skating there sometime.

Sergio Yeah. _____ .

Peter So, what's the pool there like?

Sergio Gigantic. I think it's the biggest pool _____ .

Peter Do you remember that little pool in Lincoln Park?

Sergio Yeah. We always had a lot of fun there.

Peter _____ . But it was _____ small.

Sergio Yeah, but _____ it was free. It costs $20 to swim in this new pool!

5 What do you think?

Complete the questions with superlatives. Then ask and answer the questions with a partner.

1. What's _____the tallest_____ (tall) building in this city?
2. What's _____ (nice) park around here?
3. Where's _____ (good) place to sit and watch people?
4. Where's _____ (expensive) restaurant in this city?
5. What's _____ (delicious) thing you've ever eaten?
6. What's _____ (bad) movie you've ever seen?
7. Who's _____ (busy) person you know?

6 What are they like?

A Add an appropriate adverb before each adjective below.

extremely generous   _____ talented
_____ disorganized   _____ reliable
_____ impatient   _____ arrogant

B *Pair work* Can you think of a person for each of the qualities above? Think of one thing this person is always doing. Tell a partner.

"My friend Cecilia is extremely generous. She's always helping people."

Self-check

How sure are you about these areas? Circle the percentages.

grammar
20% 40% 60% 80% 100%
vocabulary
20% 40% 60% 80% 100%
conversation strategies
20% 40% 60% 80% 100%

Study plan

What do you want to review? Circle the lessons.

grammar
1A 1B 2A 2B 3A 3B
vocabulary
1A 1B 2A 2B 3A 3B
conversation strategies
1C 2C 3C

Family life

In Unit 4, you learn how to . . .

- use *let*, *make*, *help*, *have*, *get*, *want*, *ask*, and *tell* to talk about rules and discipline.
- use *used to* and *would* to talk about memories.
- talk about family, relatives, and childhood.
- give opinions with expressions like *It seems like* and *If you ask me.*
- use expressions like *definitely*, *absolutely*, etc., to agree.

Before you begin . . .

What activities do you and your family do together?
Tell the class three things.

Lesson A Family gripes

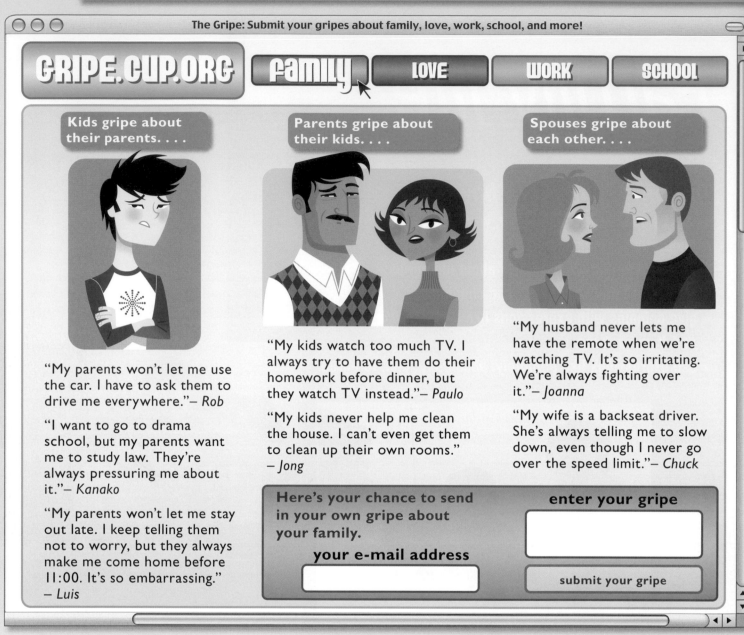

The Gripe: Submit your gripes about family, love, work, school, and more!

GRIPE.CUP.ORG | family | LOVE | WORK | SCHOOL

Kids gripe about their parents. . . .

"My parents won't let me use the car. I have to ask them to drive me everywhere."– *Rob*

"I want to go to drama school, but my parents want me to study law. They're always pressuring me about it."– *Kanako*

"My parents won't let me stay out late. I keep telling them not to worry, but they always make me come home before 11:00. It's so embarrassing." – *Luis*

Parents gripe about their kids. . . .

"My kids watch too much TV. I always try to have them do their homework before dinner, but they watch TV instead."– *Paulo*

"My kids never help me clean the house. I can't even get them to clean up their own rooms." – *Jong*

Spouses gripe about each other. . . .

"My husband never lets me have the remote when we're watching TV. It's so irritating. We're always fighting over it."– *Joanna*

"My wife is a backseat driver. She's always telling me to slow down, even though I never go over the speed limit."– *Chuck*

Here's your chance to send in your own gripe about your family.

your e-mail address

enter your gripe

submit your gripe

1 Getting started

A Read the messages on the Web site above. What problems do the people have?

> **Figure it out**

B Complete the sentences about the people above.

1. Rob's parents don't want him _____ the car.
2. Luis's parents make him _____ home before 11:00.
3. Paulo can't get his kids _____ their homework before dinner.
4. Jong's kids won't help her _____ the house.
5. Chuck's wife always tells him _____ , even when he's not driving fast.

> **About you**

C *Pair work* Do you have any gripes like the ones above? Tell a partner.

2 Grammar *Verbs let, make, help, have, get, want, ask, tell*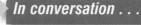

let / make / help / have + object + verb	get / want / ask / tell + object + to + verb
My parents won't **let** me **stay out** late.	I can't **get** them **to clean up** their rooms.
They **make** me **come** home before 11:00.	My parents **want** me **to study** law.
My kids never **help** me **clean** the house.	I have to **ask** them **to drive** me everywhere.
I **have** them **do** their homework before dinner.	My wife is always **telling** me **to slow down**.

A Complete the sentences with verbs.

1. When I was a kid, my parents never let me _____ to school by myself.
2. My parents made me _____ to bed at 8:00.
3. My mother couldn't get me _____ any vegetables.
4. My sister never lets me _____ her computer.
5. My parents want me _____ more time with them.
6. My wife's always telling me _____ more exercise.
7. I always have my husband _____ breakfast on the weekends.
8. I think kids should help their parents _____ the house.

> **In conversation . . .**
>
> You can also say, for example, *help me to do something*, but this is much less common.
>
>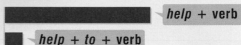

B *Pair work* Make five of the sentences above true for you. Tell a partner.

"When I was a kid, my parents never let me eat junk food."

3 Listening and speaking *Reasonable demands?*

A Parents often make demands on their children. Which of the parents' demands below do you think are reasonable? Which are not?

Parents' demands

1. Emma _____   a. get married and start a family
2. Robert _____   b. move to their neighborhood
3. Julia _____   c. work in the family business
4. Justin _____   d. call them every week

B 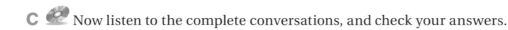 Listen to the four people above talk about their parents' demands. Each conversation is incomplete. What demand is each person talking about? Match.

C Now listen to the complete conversations, and check your answers.

D *Group work* Do your parents make any of the demands above? What other demands do they make? Tell the group.

"My parents don't want me to get married. They want me to finish college first."

1 Building vocabulary and grammar

A Listen and read the article. What memories do these people have?

HAPPIEST MEMORIES

We asked people to send us a photo and write about their happiest childhood memory.

My happiest memory is of my **great-grandmother**. She always used to keep candy in her pockets, and she'd always give us some when we came to visit. My dad used to tease us and say, "Grandma, don't give them any candy!" But she did anyway.
– Mi Soon, Seoul, South Korea

All my **aunts** and **uncles** used to come over for Sunday dinner, and there were always about 12 of us around a gigantic table. My **cousins** and I would crawl under it during dinner and play. I'm an only child, so it was nice to be part of a big **extended family**.
– Claudia, San Juan, Puerto Rico

My sister and **brother-in-law** used to live next door. I'm only a little older than my sister's kids, so I kind of grew up with my **niece** and **nephew**. I used to go over there a lot, and we'd play together. I was their favorite **uncle**!
– Hasan, Istanbul, Turkey

I used to love playing basketball with my four brothers. I grew up in a **blended family**, with two **stepbrothers** and two **half brothers**. After my parents got divorced, my father married a woman with two sons, and they had two more kids together. Anyway, the five of us used to play on a team, and we would always win.
– John, Oakland, California, U.S.A.

Word sort → **B** Complete the chart with male or female family members. Then tell a partner about your family.

Immediate family		Extended family		Blended family	
father	mother		great-grandmother	stepfather	
	sister	grandfather			stepsister
husband			aunt	stepson	
	daughter	cousin			half sister
			niece		
		brother-in-law			

"I don't have any brothers or sisters, but I have three cousins and two aunts."

Figure it out → **C** Find all the examples of *used to* and *would* or *'d* in the article. Do you think these activities and situations are finished or still continue?

2 Grammar *used to and would*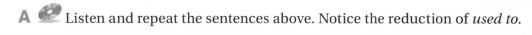

> **Use used to for regular activities or situations in the past that don't happen now or are no longer true.**
>
> I **used to go** over to my sister's house a lot. →
> My grandmother **used to keep** candy in her pockets. →
> The five of us **used to play** on a team. →
>
> **Negatives and questions with used to are less common.**
>
> I **didn't use to** like jazz.
> What kind of music **did** you **use to** like?
>
> **Use would for regular activities in the past.**
>
> I**'d play** with my niece and nephew.
> She**'d** always **give** us some.
> We **would** always **win**.
>
> **Don't use would for situations in the past.**
>
> My sister **used to** live next door.
> (NOT ~~My sister would live next door.~~)

About you → What family memories do you have? Complete each sentence, and add a sentence with *would*. Then compare your memories with a partner.

> *In conversation . . .*
>
> People often begin a story with **used to** and then continue with **would**.

When I was a kid, . . .

1. My family used to go ___to the beach___ in the summer. *We'd go almost every weekend.*
2. My mother used to make _____ for us.
3. My brother / sister and I used to play _____ together.
4. My family used to watch _____ on TV.
5. I used to see my aunts, uncles, and cousins _____ .
6. My grandparents used to take me to _____ .
7. My family always used to _____ on Sundays.

A My family used to go to the beach in the summer. We'd go almost every weekend.

B Really? I bet that was fun. My family used to visit my grandmother. . . .

3 Speaking naturally *used to*

> /yuwstə/
> *We **used to** visit my great-grandmother.*   *I **used to** play with my cousins.*

A Listen and repeat the sentences above. Notice the reduction of *used to*.

B Now listen and repeat these sentences.

1. I used to love playing hide-and-seek.
2. I used to hate broccoli.
3. I used to be afraid of the dark.
4. We used to have a goldfish.
5. My sister used to tease me a lot.

About you → **C** *Pair work* Tell a partner five things about yourself as a child. Use *used to*.

"When I was a child, I used to love playing tic-tac-toe."   *"Me too. And I also used to like . . ."*

4 Vocabulary notebook *Remember that?*

See page 42 for a useful way to log and learn vocabulary.

Lesson C If you ask me, . . .

1 Conversation strategy Giving opinions

A Which person is stating a fact? Which one is giving an opinion?

A *I read that in over half of all families, both parents work.*
B *Yeah. I don't think parents spend enough time with their children.*

Now listen. What does Paula say about her family life?

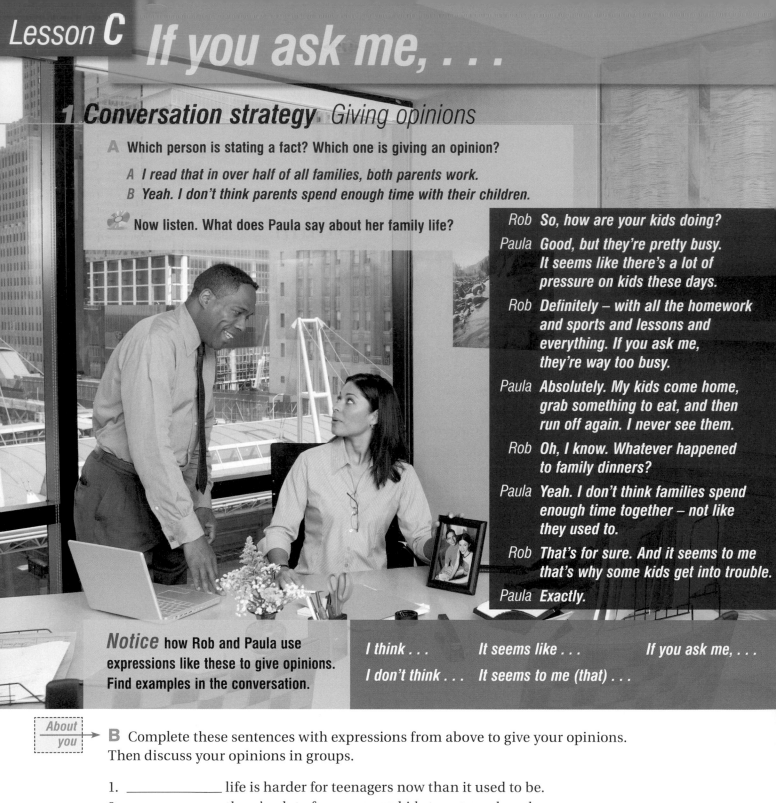

Rob So, how are your kids doing?

Paula Good, but they're pretty busy. It seems like there's a lot of pressure on kids these days.

Rob Definitely – with all the homework and sports and lessons and everything. If you ask me, they're way too busy.

Paula Absolutely. My kids come home, grab something to eat, and then run off again. I never see them.

Rob Oh, I know. Whatever happened to family dinners?

Paula Yeah. I don't think families spend enough time together – not like they used to.

Rob That's for sure. And it seems to me that's why some kids get into trouble.

Paula Exactly.

Notice how Rob and Paula use expressions like these to give opinions. Find examples in the conversation.

| I think . . . | It seems like . . . | If you ask me, . . . |
| I don't think . . . | It seems to me (that) . . . | |

About you

B Complete these sentences with expressions from above to give your opinions. Then discuss your opinions in groups.

1. _____ life is harder for teenagers now than it used to be.
2. _____ there's a lot of pressure on kids to get good grades.
3. _____ teachers should give students less homework.
4. _____ kids should spend more time with their parents.
5. _____ teenagers get into more trouble these days than they used to.
6. _____ television is a bad influence on children these days.
7. _____ kids should spend less time on the Internet.

A *It seems to me that life is harder for teenagers now than it used to be.*
B *I agree. I think that kids today have a lot of choices to make.*
C *I don't know. If you ask me, they're pretty lucky.*

SELF-STUDY
AUDIO CD
CD-ROM

2 Strategy plus Agreeing

You can use these expressions to agree with people's opinions.

Absolutely.	You're right.	I agree (with you).
Definitely.	That's true.	(Oh,) yeah.
Exactly.	That's for sure.	(Oh,) I know.

If you ask me, they're way too busy.

Absolutely.

Listen. Write the responses these people use to agree. Then practice the conversations with a partner.

In conversation . . .

Exactly, **definitely**, and **absolutely** are in the top 600 words.

1. A It seems like people are getting married much later these days.
   B _____ I think it's better to wait until you're older.
   A _____ That way you have time to grow up.

2. A I think it's sad that so many people get divorced these days.
   B _____ I heard that 1 in 3 marriages ends in divorce. That's terrible, especially when kids are involved.
   A _____ It's a real shame.

3. A It's too bad families don't eat together anymore.
   B _____ I read an article about that. It said when families eat together, the kids get into less trouble because they talk to each other more.
   A _____ And anyway, it's just nicer to eat together.

4. A You know, I don't think it's good when both parents work. It's not good for the kids.
   B _____ But I guess some families need two incomes.
   A _____ But money isn't everything.

3 Talk about it Ideal families

Group work Discuss the questions. Which topics do you agree on? Tell the class.

► Are people getting married later these days?
► What's the best age to get married? to start a family?
► Do you think families should spend more time together?
► How important is it for families to eat together? Why?
► Is it bad for children when both parents work?
► Do you think it's important for children to spend time with their grandparents?

4 Free talk Family histories

See **Free talk 4** for more speaking practice.

1 Reading

A When you were a kid, did you argue with family members? What about?
Tell the class.

B Read Rhonda's blog. Why did Rhonda and her brother use to argue?

Rhonda's Blog

RHONDA'S RAMBLINGS

| Home | About Me | Archives | Links |

11/9/2004
Childhood memories

Kids always have to sit in the backseat these days. They can't sit in the front seat, because every car now has air bags, and kids might get hurt by these safety devices.

This would have taken a lot of the joy away from my childhood. How many times did my brother and I fight over who got to sit in front? I'm surprised my mom never really implemented a policy. She kind of left it up to us. Once in a while, she would put her foot down and make us take turns. Otherwise, it was a free-for-all. "All" being my brother and I. I recall that at times, the front seat would go to whoever yelled "I call the front!" first. But it had to be after we were outside of the store or the house. We couldn't "call it" while we were still inside.

Sometimes we would determine who got to sit in the front by whoever touched the car first. I inevitably lost in this one because my brother was older and more athletic, and therefore quicker. So, he would tag the car first.

And the other way we would decide who got the front was by arguing over whose turn it was. Of course, we always thought it was our own turn. So, we'd argue about it until one of us gave in, or my mom got frustrated enough to make one of us sit in the back.

Kids nowadays don't even know what they are missing. For my brother and me, fighting over the front seat was an important part of our sibling bonding.

Source: *Rhonda's Ramblings*

C Find the expressions on the left in the blog. Match each one with a similar expression.

1. implemented a policy _____   a. demanded something strongly
2. left it up to us _____   b. forming a close relationship with a brother / sister
3. put her foot down _____   c. agreed to someone's demand
4. free-for-all _____   d. made a set of rules
5. gave in _____   e. let us decide what to do
6. sibling bonding _____   f. a competition with no rules

D Read the blog again. For each statement below, check true or false. Correct the false statements. Then compare ideas with a partner.

	True	False
1. Rhonda's mother always decided who would ride in the front seat.	☐	☐
2. Rhonda and her brother had rules for deciding who rode in the front seat.	☐	☐
3. If Rhonda yelled "I call the front!" inside the house, she could ride in front.	☐	☐
4. Rhonda would usually touch the car before her brother.	☐	☐
5. Rhonda and her brother always thought it was their turn to ride in front.	☐	☐

2 *Listening and writing* Family activities

A Listen. What did these people use to do? Number the pictures.

B Listen again. Why don't the people do these things now? Write a reason under each picture.

About you

C *Group work* Think of three things you used to do with your family. Tell your group.

A We used to ski every winter, but my dad hurt his knee, so we stopped.
B Really? My parents didn't let us go skiing because they thought it was too dangerous.

D Choose a family memory from your childhood. Write a blog about it.

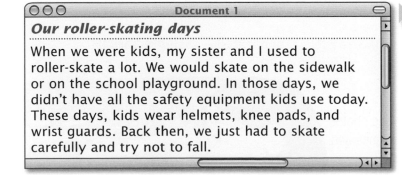

Help note

Using time markers

- Use these time markers to show the past:
  When we were kids, . . . / When I was . . .
  In those days, . . . / Back then, . . .

- Use these time markers to show the present:
  today, now, nowadays, these days

E *Group work* Read your classmates' blogs. Then ask questions to find out more information.

"How far did you use to skate?"   *"Did your parents let you skate by yourselves?"*

Vocabulary notebook

Remember that?

Learning tip Word webs

Use word webs to log new vocabulary about your family members.
What memories do you associate with each person?

1 Look at the picture. Complete the word web with memories of the grandfather in the picture.

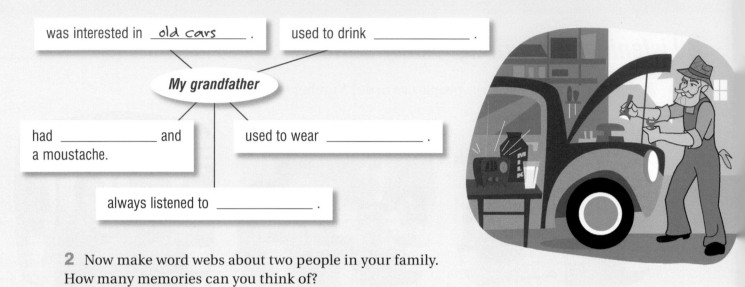

| was interested in _old cars_ . | used to drink _____ . |

My grandfather

| had _____ and a moustache. | used to wear _____ . |

always listened to _____ .

2 Now make word webs about two people in your family.
How many memories can you think of?

3 *Word builder* Do you know this vocabulary? Find out the meanings of any words
you don't know. Can you add any of the words to your word webs?

adopted   **ex-husband**   **great-aunt**   **separated**   **single parent**

On your own

Make a photo album of your family. Find photos
of each of your relatives. Write their names and
a short memory about each picture.

Aunt Emily and me
We used to bake cookies

42

Food choices

In Unit 5, you learn how to . . .

- talk about food using expressions like *a bottle of*, *a quart of*, *a loaf of*, etc.
- use quantifiers like *a little*, *a few*, *very little*, and *very few*.
- use *too*, *too much*, *too many*, and *enough*.
- talk about eating habits and different ways to cook food.
- respond to suggestions by letting the other person decide.
- refuse offers politely using expressions like *No, thanks. I'm fine*.

Before you begin . . .

Can you find these foods in the picture? What other foods can you find? Have you bought any of these things recently?

- a bag of potato chips
- a bottle of ketchup
- a package of frozen peas
- some cartons of juice
- a box of cereal
- a jar of mustard
- a can of soup

Healthy food

What do you have in your refrigerator?

We visited three people to see what they keep in the fridge.

> Let's see, um, a carton of eggs, a quart of milk, a pound of hamburger, a few slices of cheese, and a little butter. Um, there aren't many vegetables. There are just a few green peppers going bad in the vegetable bin. I guess I should eat more vegetables.
>
> — *David Freeman*

> Well, there's very little food in there because I eat out most nights. So there's just a loaf of bread, a bottle of soy sauce, and a jar of hot peppers. Yeah, there's not much food in the house.
>
> — *Chris Kim*

> Oh, there's lots of stuff. There's fruit – oranges, mangoes, a pineapple. And I always have plenty of fresh vegetables – broccoli, tomatoes, and carrots. And there's some milk. I usually buy skim milk because it has fewer calories. And then in the freezer there are one or two frozen dinners, but not many. We eat very few frozen meals.
>
> — *Marta Delgado*

1 Getting started

A 💿 Listen. Who has the healthiest food in the refrigerator?

> **Figure it out**

B Read about the people, and look inside the refrigerators. Each person forgot to mention two things. What did they forget? Use these expressions.

a bottle of   a jar of   a loaf of   a few   a little   a quart of

"David also has a bottle of ketchup in his refrigerator. And he has . . ."

2 Grammar *Talking about quantities of food*

Uncountable nouns	Countable nouns
We have **a little** butter in the fridge. = *some*	We have **a few** slices of cheese. = *some*
There's **very little** food. = *not a lot*	We eat **very few** frozen meals. = *not a lot*
I'm trying to eat **less** fat.	Skim milk has **fewer** calories.
There's **not much** food in the house.	There are**n't many** vegetables.

very little / very few = not a lot

Food containers / items	Weights and measures	
a carton of juice → two cartons of juice	a liter of / a quart of	*1 liter = 1.1 quarts*
a loaf of bread → two loaves of bread	a kilo of / a pound of	*1 kilo = 2.2 pounds*
		kilo = kilogram

About you → Add food items to make each sentence true for you. Then compare information with a partner.

1. In my refrigerator, there's a jar of _____ , a bottle of _____ ,
   and a liter of _____ .
2. In my cupboard, there's probably a bag of _____ , a package of _____ ,
   and a can of _____ .
3. I eat a few _____ and a little _____ every week.
4. I've bought very little _____ and very few _____ recently.
5. I probably should eat fewer _____ and more _____ .
6. I eat less _____ than I used to.
7. Yesterday, I ate a little _____ and a few _____ , but I didn't eat
   much _____ .
8. I'm not eating many _____ these days.

A In my refrigerator, there's a jar of mayonnaise, . . .
B We don't eat mayonnaise, but we have some jars of jam and some curry paste.

3 Talk about it *Is it good for you?*

Group work Look at these beliefs about food. Discuss each one. Do you agree?

It's good to eat a few **NUTS** every day. They're very healthy.

Eating **LESS FOOD** can help you **LIVE LONGER**.

A little **CHOCOLATE** can be good for you. It can improve your mood.

You should try to eat nine portions of **FRESH FRUIT** and **VEGETABLES** every day.

If you eat fewer **CARBOHYDRATES** and a little more **FAT** and **PROTEIN**, you will lose weight more quickly.

A cup of **GREEN TEA** every day is good for your general health.

A Did you know it's good to eat a few nuts every day?
B No, I didn't. I don't eat many nuts, actually. They have a lot of fat in them.

Lesson B A question of taste

1 Building vocabulary

A Have you eaten any of these foods recently? Which ones do you like best?

(stir-)fried noodles	**grilled** shrimp	**steamed** vegetables	**boiled** eggs	**baked** potatoes

pickled cabbage	**roast** lamb	**barbecued** beef	**raw** fish	**smoked** fish

Word sort

B How do you like to eat different foods? Complete the chart. What would you like to eat tonight? Tell the class.

Notice . . .
Adjective
fried, grilled, . . .
Verb
fry, grill, . . .

fried	grilled	steamed	boiled	baked	roast(ed)	barbecued
eggs	fish					
potatoes						

2 Speaking naturally *Stressing new information*

A Do you like fried rice?   B Yes, I love fried rice.   **or**   B Actually, I prefer steamed rice.

A Do you like raw fish?   B Yes, I love raw fish.   **or**   B I've never tried raw fish.

A Have you ever eaten raw eggs?   B Yes, I eat raw eggs for breakfast.   **or**   B No, I only eat cooked eggs.

A Listen and repeat the questions and answers above. Notice how the stress and intonation move to the new information in the answers. Then ask and answer the questions with a partner.

About you

B *Pair work* Compare charts from Exercise 1B above. How do you like your foods prepared?

"I like fried eggs. Do you?"   "No, not really. I always boil my eggs. Boiled eggs are healthier."

46

3 Building language

A  Listen. What do Carla and Leo want to order? Practice the conversation.

Carla Are you going to have dessert?

Leo No, I'm too full. I ate too many fries.

Carla Do you mind if I have something? My salad wasn't filling enough. I mean, is there enough time? I know I eat too slowly – probably because I talk too much!

Leo That's not true! Anyway, I want another iced tea. I'm really thirsty. I guess I put too much salt on my fries.

Carla OK. So I'm going to order some apple pie.

Leo Mmm. Sounds good. Maybe I'll have some, too.

Carla Well, as they say, there's always room for dessert!

 B Can you complete these sentences with *enough*, *too*, and *too much*?

1. Leo isn't hungry because he ate _____ food.

2. Carla didn't have _____ food to eat.

3. Leo is thirsty because his fries were _____ salty.

4 Grammar *too, too much, too many, and enough*

	too / too much / too many	enough
With nouns	I ate **too much food** / **too many fries**.	I didn't eat **enough food** / **fries**.
As pronouns	I ate **too much** / **too many**.	I didn't eat **enough**.
With adjectives	He's **too full**.	Her salad wasn't **filling enough**.
With adverbs	She eats **too slowly**.	She doesn't eat **fast enough**.
With verbs	She **talks too much**.	Maybe she **doesn't listen enough**.

A Complete these sentences with *too, too much, too many,* or *enough*.

1. I eat _____ fast food and not _____ fruit and vegetables.
2. I'm never hungry _____ to eat dinner because I eat _____ snacks.
3. There's never _____ time to shop or cook, so I eat out a lot.
4. During my exams, I study _____ , and I don't sleep or eat _____ .
5. I don't like smoked or pickled foods because they're _____ salty.
6. If I don't eat _____ for breakfast, I'm _____ hungry by lunchtime.
7. When I'm stressed out, I eat _____ quickly. Then I get a stomachache.
8. I think there's _____ fat in fried foods. It's better to grill them or steam them.

 B *Pair work* Are the sentences above true for you? Discuss with a partner.

A I don't eat too much fast food. I try to eat a lot of fruit and vegetables.

B That's good. I probably eat too much fast food. I don't have enough time to eat properly.

5 Vocabulary notebook *Fried bananas*

See page 52 for a new way to log and learn vocabulary.

Lesson C Whatever you're having.

1 Conversation strategy Letting another person decide

A Look at the question and answers. Which guest wants the host to make the decision?

Host **Can I get you something, like tea or coffee?**

Guest A **I'll have tea, please.**   Guest B **Either one is fine.**   Guest C **Actually, do you have any soda?**

Now listen. What does Laura offer Kayla?

Laura	**Can I get you something to eat?**
Kayla	**Oh, I'm OK for now. But thanks.**
Laura	**Are you sure? I have some cheese in the fridge and a box of crackers.**
Kayla	**No, thanks. I'm fine. Really. Maybe later.**
Laura	**Well, how about some tea or coffee?**
Kayla	**Um . . . are you having some?**
Laura	**Yeah. I need to wake up a bit. So, tea or coffee?**
Kayla	**Either one is fine. Whatever you're having.**
Laura	**OK. I think I'll make some tea. Do you want it with milk or lemon?**
Kayla	**Oh. Either way. Whichever is easier. Are you sure it's not too much trouble?**
Laura	**No, no. It's no trouble at all.**

Notice how Kayla uses expressions like these because she wants Laura to decide. Find examples in the conversation.

Either one (is fine).
Either way (is fine).

Whatever you're having.
Whichever is easier (for you).
Whatever you prefer.

B *Pair work* Write a response to these questions, letting the other person decide. Then practice the conversations with a partner.

1. "I'm thirsty. I could make us some lemonade or some iced tea. What would you like?"
2. "There are two good movies at the Plaza Theater, *Life of Crime* and *Crazy Love*. Which one do you want to see?"
3. "Do you want to have dinner after the movie? Or maybe meet for dinner before?"
4. "Let's buy some popcorn. Do you want it with or without butter?"
5. "Would you like to share a dessert? Maybe some apple pie or ginger ice cream?"

SELF-STUDY
AUDIO CD
CD-ROM

48

2 *Strategy plus* *Polite refusals*

You can use expressions like these to refuse offers of food and drink politely.

No, thanks. Maybe later.
No, thanks. I'm fine. Really.
I'm OK for now. But thanks.

Can I get you something to eat?

I'm OK for now. But thanks.

Imagine you are the guest at this party. How can you refuse your host's offers politely? Complete the conversation. Then practice with a partner.

Host Would you like something to eat?
Guest _____
Host Are you sure? There's a big plate of my special barbecued chicken.
Guest _____
Host Well, can I get you something cold to drink? I have juice, soda, . . .
Guest _____
Host Well, if you change your mind, just let me know.

3 *Listening* *That sounds good.*

A Listen to the conversations. Number the pictures.

B Listen again. Match each picture above with the appropriate response below to complete the conversations. Write the numbers on the lines.

a. They all look good. Whatever you prefer. _____
b. Either one is fine. Whatever you're having. _____
c. I could go either way. You choose. _____
d. No, thanks. I'm fine. Maybe later. _____

4 *Free talk* *Do we have enough for the party?*

See *Free talk 5* for more speaking practice.

1 Reading

A   Brainstorm! How many different snacks can you think of? Which ones are popular in your country? Make a class list.

B   Read the article. Which snacks do you eat? Which would you like to try?

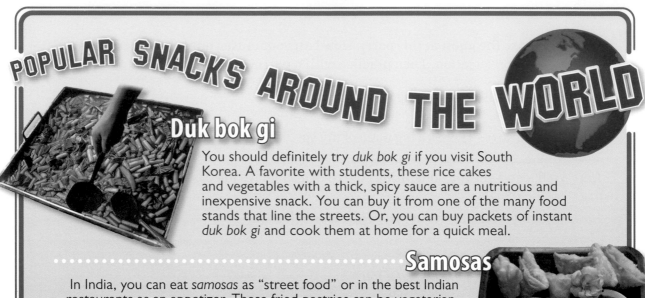

POPULAR SNACKS AROUND THE WORLD

Duk bok gi

You should definitely try *duk bok gi* if you visit South Korea. A favorite with students, these rice cakes and vegetables with a thick, spicy sauce are a nutritious and inexpensive snack. You can buy it from one of the many food stands that line the streets. Or, you can buy packets of instant *duk bok gi* and cook them at home for a quick meal.

Samosas

In India, you can eat *samosas* as "street food" or in the best Indian restaurants as an appetizer. These fried pastries can be vegetarian, with ingredients like chickpeas, lentils, and potatoes, or they can have a delicious meat filling, such as ground lamb. They are good with chutney (a thick sauce containing chopped fruit, vinegar, sugar, and spices).

Falafel

Another favorite "street food," *falafel*, is popular throughout the Middle East. *Falafel* is a mixture of ground chickpeas with onion, garlic, and other spices shaped into balls or patties and deep-fried. People often eat *falafel* with yogurt or tahini (sesame seed paste).

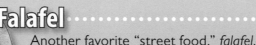

Popcorn

Over 2,000 years ago, native peoples of North and South America ate popcorn. They heated a type of corn over a fire until it "popped," or burst open. You can make popcorn by heating it in oil. Or pop it without oil to make a low-calorie snack — unless, of course, you add melted butter! Today, people in the United States eat over one billion pounds of popcorn per year.

French fries

No one is absolutely sure about the origin of French fries, with both France and Belgium claiming the invention of these delicious strips of potatoes deep-fried in oil. In recent years, fast-food chains in countries all over the world have probably made French fries one of the world's most popular snacks. Everyone has a favorite way of eating them, for example, with ketchup, mayonnaise, vinegar, or just salt.

C Read the article again. Complete the chart for each snack.

Name of snack	Popular in . . .	Ingredients	Good with . . .
duk bok gi	South Korea	rice and vegetables	spicy sauce

2 *Listening and speaking* Snack habits

A  Listen. What snacks are the people talking about? Number the pictures.

	peanuts

	pizza

	ice cream

B Listen again. How would each person answer the questions? Complete the chart.

	Catherine	Josh	Zoe
1. What's your favorite snack food?			
2. How often do you eat this snack?			
3. Do you think this snack is healthy? Why?			

 About you

C *Group work* Discuss the questions above. Complete a chart like the one above with your classmates' information. Which of the snacks are healthy?

3 *Writing* You should definitely try it!

A *Pair work* Choose a snack food or traditional dish popular in your country. Write an article about it for a tourist pamphlet. Use the article on page 50 to help you. Include a photo if you can.

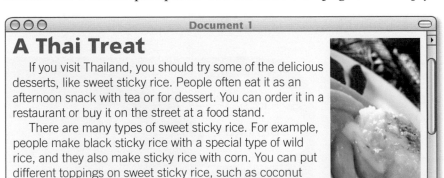

○○○ Document 1

A Thai Treat

If you visit Thailand, you should try some of the delicious desserts, like sweet sticky rice. People often eat it as an afternoon snack with tea or for dessert. You can order it in a restaurant or buy it on the street at a food stand.

There are many types of sweet sticky rice. For example, people make black sticky rice with a special type of wild rice, and they also make sticky rice with corn. You can put different toppings on sweet sticky rice, such as coconut custard, fresh coconut cream, and fresh mangoes.

Help note

Giving examples

You can introduce examples with:
like
for example
such as

B *Pair work* Read a partner's article. Can you add any more information?

Vocabulary notebook

Fried bananas

Learning tip *Collocations – words that go together*

When you learn new words, learn them in combination with other words. For example, learn adjectives that can go before a particular noun.

> boiled eggs, fried eggs, raw eggs

Talk about eating

The most common collocations in conversation with these 6 cooking words are:

1. *fried* chicken   4. *grilled* cheese
2. *boiled* eggs   5. *smoked* salmon
3. *baked* potatoes   6. *raw* fish

1 Cross out the adjective that doesn't go well with each noun.

a. fried
pickled
~~smoked~~ — onions
raw

b. barbecued
steamed
fried — rice
boiled

c. stir-fried
spicy
boiled — noodles
pickled

d. smoked
fresh
canned — fruit
dried

2 How many cooking or taste words can you put before these foods? List them from your favorite to your least favorite ways of eating them.

least favorite	- - - - - - - - - - → favorite			
grilled				fish
				chicken
				eggs
				red peppers
				pineapple
				carrots

3 *Word builder* Which adjective goes best with each noun? Complete the expressions.

✓creamed   dark   grated   mashed   scrambled   sweet and sour   whole   whole wheat

_____ eggs   _____ shrimp   _____ chocolate   _____ bread
_____ milk   _creamed_ spinach   _____ potatoes   _____ cheese

On your own

The next time you go to or pass a restaurant, look at the menu. Translate 5 of the dishes into English.

Fried bananas.

52

Managing life

In Unit 6, you learn how to . . .

- use *will*, *going to*, the present continuous, and the simple present to talk about the future.
- talk about future plans, facts, predictions, and schedules.
- use *ought to*, *have got to*, *would rather*, *had better*, and *going to have to*.
- talk about what's advisable, what's necessary, and what's preferable.
- use expressions with *make* and *do*.
- end phone conversations and use informal expressions to say good-bye.

1

2

3

Before you begin . . .

How good are you at managing your life? Are you good at . . .

- ☐ organizing your social life?
- ☐ dealing with problems at work or school?
- ☐ keeping your house neat and organized?

Hello?

• • • • • • • • •

Oh, hi, Brandon. How are you?

• • • • • • • • •

Good, really good. . . . No, it's OK. I'm on my way home.

• • • • • • • • •

What am I doing tomorrow night? Actually, I don't think I'm doing anything. . . .

• • • • • • • • •

Oh, wait. Tomorrow's Tuesday. I have my aerobics class. That starts at 7:00, and then I'm meeting Anna afterwards. We're going to have dinner together. But, yeah, I'd love to catch up with you. How about Wednesday night?

• • • • • • • • •

Huh. So you're going to be out of town for a couple of days, . . . but you'll be back Friday, right? So what about Friday?

• • • • • • • • •

Uh-oh. I just remembered. My boss is going to have us all work late Friday. She mentioned it last week. We have this big deadline.

• • • • • • • • •

Yeah, yeah. We won't be finished on time. It's a long story. Uh, I'll tell you about it sometime.

• • • • • • • • •

Tonight? Actually, I'm not doing anything!

• • • • • • • • •

That's a fabulous idea. I'll just stop by my apartment to change clothes, and then I'll come right over to meet you. I can get there by 7:30. And I'll call for a reservation.

• • • • • • • • •

Great. So, see you in about an hour. Bye.

1 Getting started

A 💿 Listen. Stacy is talking to her friend Brandon. When do they decide to meet? Can you guess what they're going to do?

Figure it out

B How would Stacy say these things to Brandon? Use the conversation above, and choose the best verb forms.

1. "Anna and I **will** / **are going to** have dinner tomorrow night."
2. "My guess is that **we're not meeting** / **we won't meet** our deadline on Friday."
3. "**I'm not doing** / **I won't do** anything tonight. So let's get together."

2 Grammar Talking about the future

Use **will** when you decide to do something as you are speaking.	I'**ll** just stop by my apartment to change clothes, and then I'**ll** come right over to meet you.
Use **will** or **going to** for factual information or predictions based on what you know.	You're **going to be** out of town, but you'**ll** be back Friday? My boss **is going to** make us work late Friday. Our project **won't** be finished on time.
Use the present continuous or **going to** (not **will**) for decisions you've made and fixed plans.	I'**m meeting** Anna after my aerobics class. We'**re going to** have dinner together. I'**m not doing** anything tonight.
Use the simple present for schedules.	I **have** my aerobics class tomorrow. It **starts** at 7:00.

Complete the conversations with appropriate ways to talk about the future, using the words given. There are two possible answers in many cases. Practice with a partner.

1. *A* I _____ (have) a little party at my place Friday night. Can you come?
   B Actually, I _____ (go) to the basketball game. It _____ (start) at 8:00.
   So I don't think it _____ (be) over until after 9:00. Is that too late?
   A Not at all. My guess is that most people _____ (not arrive) until 9:00 or 9:30.
   B Great. So I _____ (come) over right after the game.

2. *A* What _____ (you / do) tomorrow night?
   B Well, I _____ (go) shopping for some shoes. But I'm free after that.
   A When _____ you _____ (be) finished? Do you know?
   B By 8:00. Then we can meet at the coffee shop.

3. *A* _____ (you / go out) for lunch?
   B Well, I _____ (go) to the bank, but I'm not sure about lunch. How about you?
   A I don't know. I think I _____ (have) lunch outside somewhere.
   Do you want to come with me? It _____ (be) nice to sit in the sun.
   B OK. I _____ (finish) this e-mail, and then I _____ (be) ready to go.

3 Listening and speaking *I hope you can come.*

A Listen to these people responding to invitations. Complete the chart. Which event sounds the most interesting?

	Martin	**Julia**	**Rachel**
What's the invitation for?	a concert		
When is it?	Monday at 7:00 p.m.		
What are his / her plans then?			
What does he / she decide to do?			

B *Pair work* Role-play a situation like the ones above. Student A: Invite your partner to do something on a specific day. Student B: Tell your partner your plans for that day, and make a decision about what to do.

Problems and solutions

1 Building vocabulary and grammar

A Read the life coach's Web page. Complete the expressions with the correct form of *do* or *make*. Then listen and check your answers.

Ask the Life Coach

Do you have a personal problem that you'd rather not discuss with friends or family? Get some confidential advice from our online life coach.

Q1 Sometimes I think I ought to ___do___ **some volunteer work** in a school or a hospital, but I'm too busy just trying to _____ **a living**. I have very little free time, so I think I'd better not add anything to my schedule right now. Am I right?

*Don't _____ **excuses**. You don't have to spend all your free time doing volunteer work – three hours a week is enough. _____ **some research** and find an organization where you feel you can _____ **a difference** and _____ **some good** for other people.*

Q2 My boss is a bully. He yells at me if I _____ **a mistake**, and he _____ **fun of** me in front of my co-workers. I've tried talking to him, but it doesn't _____ **any good**. He won't listen. I guess I'm going to have to _____ **something** about this problem, but what?

*It doesn't _____ **any sense** to ignore this problem, and you'd better do something quickly before it gets worse. _____ **an appointment** with your Human Resources representative. You might want to take a colleague with you, too.*

Q3 I'm meeting my girlfriend's parents for the first time next weekend. They've invited me for dinner. I'm going to _____ **my best** to _____ **a good impression** on them, but I'm really nervous. Any advice?

*_____ **an effort** to dress nicely, and _____ **sure** you take them a small gift, such as flowers or chocolates. _____ **some nice comments** about their home, the food, etc., but don't overdo it. You ought to let them _____ **the talking** at first. The most important thing, however, is just to be yourself.*

Q4 My boss recently offered me a promotion. I've _____ **a lot of thinking** about it, but I can't _____ **up my mind** if I should take it. Sometimes I think I'd rather stay in my current job. I've got to decide by next week. What should I do?

*_____ **a list** of the pros and cons of each job, and give each one a score from 1 to 5 (5 = the best). Then _____ **the math** – add up the points for each list, and subtract the con totals from the pro totals. Which job has the highest score? Does that help you _____ **a decision**?*

B *Pair work* Do you agree with the life coach's answers? What advice can you add?

Word sort

C Make word webs for *do* and *make*. Add other expressions you know. Then compare with a partner.

Figure it out

D Find expressions on the Web page with the same meaning as the underlined words below.

1. I <u>should</u> do some volunteer work.
2. I'd <u>prefer to</u> stay in the same job.
3. I <u>have to</u> make a decision soon.
4. You <u>really should</u> do something quickly.

2 Grammar *What's advisable / necessary / preferable*

What's advisable	You'**d better** do something quickly. (*'d = had*)
	I'**d better not** add anything to my schedule.
	I **ought to** do some volunteer work.
	You **ought to** let them do the talking.
	You **might want to** take a colleague with you.
What's necessary	I'm **going to have to** do something about it.
	I'**ve got to** decide by next week. (*'ve = have*)
	You **don't have to** spend time on this.
What's preferable	I'**d rather (not)** stay in my current job. (*'d = would*)

> **In conversation . . .**
>
> **Should** is more common than **ought to** or **had better**.
>
> ███████ **should**
>
> █ **ought to**
>
> █ **had better**

About you

Pair work Complete the conversations with problems and solutions. Then practice.

1. *A* I ought to _____ tonight, but I'd rather _____ .
   B You know, I think you'd better _____ because _____ .

2. *A* I've got to make up my mind if I want to _____ .
   B That's a hard decision to make. You might want to _____ .

3. *A* I ought to make an effort to _____ every day, but it takes so much time.
   B Well, you don't have to _____ , but you ought to _____ .

4. *A* I have a friend who makes fun of me all the time, but I'd rather not _____ .
   B It won't do any good to wait. I think you're going to have to _____ .

A **I ought to study for our English test tonight, but I'd rather go to a movie.**
B **You know, I think you'd better study because that test is very important.**

3 Speaking naturally *Reduction of verbs*

You might **want to** try a new instructor. (= **wanna**)	You **ought to** take more lessons. (= **oughta**)
You'd **better** study the driver's manual. (= **you better**)	You'**ve got to** pay attention! (= **gotta**)
You're **going to have to** practice more. (= **gonna hafta**)	

Listen and repeat the sentences above. Notice the reduction of the verbs. Can you guess who this advice is for? Can you think of other advice?

4 Talk about it *What's your advice?*

Group work Who has to do any of these things soon? Discuss each one and offer advice.

- ▶ make a big decision
- ▶ make an appointment to see someone
- ▶ make an excuse to a friend
- ▶ do some thinking about your future
- ▶ make a good impression on someone
- ▶ do something about a problem at work or school
- ▶ do some good for the community
- ▶ get a job and make a living for yourself

5 Vocabulary notebook *Do your best!*

See page 62 for a useful way to log and learn vocabulary.

I've got to get going.

1 Conversation strategy *Ending phone conversations*

A How do you end phone conversations in your language? Do you use expressions like these?

> *I'd better go.*   *I've got to run.*   *Talk to you later.*   *Bye now.*

Now listen. Why can't Ling talk longer on the phone?

Ramon	**Hi, Ling. It's Ramon. Is this a good time to talk?**
Ling	**Um, not really. I'm late for a seminar. I'm going to have to run.**
Ramon	**Oh, OK. I just wanted to ask about this weekend.**
Ling	**Well, can I call you back tonight? I've got to get going.**
Ramon	**OK. I'll be home after 8:00. I'm going to the gym after work.**
Ling	**Oh, good. I'll call you later. I'd better go now.**
Ramon	**Yeah. So, think about what you want to do on Saturday.**
Ling	**Yeah, I will. Listen, Ramon, I've really got to go. I'm already late.**
Ramon	**All right. I'll let you go. By the way, what's your seminar about?**
Ling	**Being assertive. Bye now!**
Ramon	**Oh, OK! Talk to you later.**

ASSERTIVENESS SEMINAR

4TH FLOOR

Notice how Ling tries to end the phone conversation with expressions like these. Find examples in the conversation.

> *I'd better go.*
> *I've got to get going.*
> *I'm going to have to run.*

> *Can I call you back?*
> *I'll call you later.*
> *I've really got to go.*

B *Pair work* Role-play phone conversations. Student A: Call your partner about one of these topics, and try to keep the conversation going. Student B: Try to end the conversation, using the expressions above. Then change roles.

- plans for the weekend
- how your week is going
- something you're looking forward to

- something you want to borrow
- some exciting news
- something you're busy with

SELF-STUDY
AUDIO CD
CD-ROM

2 **Strategy plus** *"Friendly" good-byes*

In friendly or informal phone conversations, you can use short expressions like these to say good-bye. The words in parentheses are usually dropped.

(I'll) Talk to you later.
(I'll) Catch you later.
(I'll) See you later.
I('ve) got to go. / (I've) Got to go.
I('d) better go.
(It was) Nice talking to you.

Talk to you later.

▶ **In conversation . . .**

The shorter forms of these expressions are more common.

See you later.

I'll / We'll see you later.

Talk to you later.

I'll / We'll talk to you later.

Write the shorter forms of the underlined expressions to make these conversations more informal. Then practice the conversations with a partner.

1. *A* Hi, it's me. Are you coming on Saturday?
   B Yeah. I'll be there. Can't wait.
   A All right. <u>I'll see you Saturday.</u>

2. *A* Anyway, I'm at work, so <u>I'd better go.</u>
   B OK. <u>I'll talk to you later.</u>
   A Yeah. <u>I've got to go. I'll see you.</u>

3. *A* OK, well, <u>I'd better let you go.</u>
   B Yeah. <u>It was good talking to you.</u>
   A Yeah. Take care. Bye.

4. *A* Listen, my bus is coming. <u>I'll catch you later.</u>
   B Yeah. <u>I've got to go</u> anyway.
   A <u>I'll see you tomorrow.</u> Bye.

3 **Talk about it** *Phone habits*

Group work Discuss the questions. What kind of phone habits do you have?

▶ Do you usually answer the phone, or do you let the answering machine take a message?
▶ How often do you check your phone messages? Do you call people back right away?
▶ Do you have caller ID? Do you check who's calling before you answer the phone?
▶ Do you ever make up an excuse to end a phone conversation?
▶ Do you mind if people talk on the phone when you're with them?
▶ Do you ever talk on the phone when you're with other people?
▶ Do you turn off your cell phone when you're in a movie theater? What about in class? at a friend's house? at work?
▶ How many phone numbers do you have in your cell phone's memory?

1 Reading

A Brainstorm! What does the word *clutter* make you think of? Make a word web. Then tell the class one of your words and why you chose it.

pack rat ——— clutter ——— old clothes
                        ——— spring

*"I chose the expression **pack rat** because I am one! I keep everything."*

B Read the article. Have you ever used any of these ideas for getting rid of clutter?

GETTING RID OF CLUTTER

We all live with some clutter, but getting rid of it can change your life. You'll feel more in control, you'll waste less time looking for things, and you'll be able to make room for new things in your life. But where do you start? Try this idea.

THE FOUR-BOX METHOD

Decide on an area you want to clean up. Then get three boxes and a large trash can. Label the boxes "Put Away," "Give Away / Sell," and "Store." The trash can is for the things you decide to throw away.

Take the four containers to the cleanup area. Pick up each piece of clutter, and ask yourself, "Do I want to put this away where I usually keep it, donate it or sell it, store it, or put it in the trash can?" Do not put the item down until you have made a decision!

When you have sorted all the clutter, empty the three boxes. Put back the items in the Put Away box where they usually go. Load the Give Away / Sell box in your car so you can drop it off at a friend's house or a charity donation center. List the contents of the Store box, and put it in your storage area. Finally, empty the trash can. As long as you do it immediately, you won't be able to change your mind!

YOUR CLUTTER QUESTIONS ANSWERED

Q: I have an old personal CD player that I don't use, but I can't bear to throw it out.

a: *Unless it's a collector's item or a museum piece, it's just taking up space. Let's face it – you're never going to use it, and it shows your age! Give it away or junk it.*

Q: What should I do with all my boxes of old photos? They take up so much space.

a: *You probably never look at them, either! Here's what you ought to do. Sort them into three piles. Put the fabulous shots into photo albums, and display them on your coffee table. Put the blurred, torn, and unrecognizable ones in the trash. Send the rest to friends and relatives.*

Q: I have hundreds of books that I've saved through the years. How can I part with them?

a: *Unless the books are favorites that you want to read again someday, they're junk. Take them to a used bookstore, and make yourself a bit of money. After all, one person's trash is another person's treasure!*

Q: I inherited a lot of costume jewelry from my great-grandmother. What should I do with it?

a: *Wear it! Or pass it on to your kids to use for playing dress-up. They'll love it.*

C Find the words and expressions in the article. Match them with the definitions.

1. get rid of ___
2. make room for ___
3. put away ___
4. store ___
5. donate ___

a. give (something) away to a person or an organization that can use it
b. make space for
c. put (something) in a special place for a long period of time
d. return (something) to the place where you usually keep it
e. remove (something) by giving it away or throwing it away

D Read the article again. Answer the questions. Then discuss your ideas with a partner.

1. According to the article, what are three advantages of getting rid of clutter?
2. What are four basic things the article suggests people can do with clutter?
3. What does the article say you should do with an old personal CD player? a fabulous photo? costume jewelry?
4. What is the meaning of the saying "one person's trash is another person's treasure"? Do you agree?

2 *Listening and writing* *What should I do with these?*

A You don't want these things anymore. What can you do with them? Make a class list.

① clothes   **②** games and toys   **③** magazines

B Listen to three people talk about the things above. Check (✓) what they do.

①
- ☐ *Give them to friends.*
- ☐ *Dye them a new color.*
- ☐ *Make something with them.*

②
- ☐ *Give them to a school.*
- ☐ *Sell them at a yard sale.*
- ☐ *Sell them on the Internet.*

③
- ☐ *Recycle them.*
- ☐ *Give them to the library.*
- ☐ *Give them to a neighbor.*

C Write a question about a clutter problem you have. Then exchange papers and answer your classmate's question. Give advice. Be creative.

> My parents have kept every birthday card I've ever received in a huge box! Now I'm moving into my own apartment, and I don't want to take them with me. But I hate to get rid of them. Any ideas?

Birthday cards

Most people throw away old birthday cards unless they are from someone special. But you can do some fun things with them. For example, you can make new cards with pictures from the old birthday cards. That way you can recycle the old cards and use them for someone else's birthday — as long as you don't send a card to the original sender!

Help note

Linking ideas with *as long as, provided that,* **and** *unless*

- **As long as** and **provided that** mean "if" or "only if." It's easy to recycle gifts **as long as** you remember who gave you which gift!

- **Unless** means "except if" or "if . . . not." Throw it away **unless** it's from someone special.

3 *Free talk* *Who's going to do what?*

See *Free talk 6* for more speaking practice.

Do your best!

Learning tip *Writing sentences to show meaning*

When you learn a new expression, use it in a sentence to help you remember it. Add another sentence to clarify or paraphrase the meaning.

> My brother can't make a living as a musician.
> He doesn't earn enough money.

1 Complete the sentences with these expressions.

do my best	make a difference	make a good impression	make up my mind

1. I'm going to try to _____ on my new boss. I want her to have a good opinion of me.
2. I'd like to do something useful in life. I want to _____ in people's lives.
3. I can't _____ if I want to buy an MP3 player. I can't decide if I need one.
4. I find exams very stressful, but I always _____ . I try very hard to do well.

2 Write sentences to help you remember these expressions.

1. make a decision (to do something) _____
   _____

2. do some thinking (about something) _____
   _____

3. make fun of someone _____
   _____

4. do volunteer work _____
   _____

5. make an effort (to do something) _____
   _____

3 *Word builder* Which expressions below can you complete with *make*? Find appropriate verbs to complete the other expressions. Write the words on the lines.

1. _____ changes   3. _____ a dream   5. _____ a suggestion   7. _____ a walk
2. _____ a mess   4. _____ progress   6. _____ plans   8. _____ a favor

On your own

Choose 5 expressions and make a "to do" list using them. Put your list on the wall, and cross out the items as you do them.

> Make up my mind to get rid of clutter.
>
> Do something about the broken window.
>
> Make an effort to dress nicely.

1 What do you think?

A Complete these opinions with a verb or *to* + verb. Compare with a partner.

1. Parents shouldn't let teenagers __watch__ violent shows on TV.
2. Parents ought to make their kids _____ books every night.
3. Teachers ask students _____ too much homework.
4. Parents shouldn't help their children _____ their homework.
5. Parents shouldn't let their children _____ too much junk food.
6. Parents should get their kids _____ more vegetables and fewer sweets.
7. We shouldn't let young people _____ cars until they're 21.
8. We ought to ask all teenagers _____ some volunteer work.

B *Group work* Discuss three or four opinions above. Use the expressions in the boxes to give your opinions and to show when you agree.

A If you ask me, parents shouldn't let teenagers watch violent shows on TV.

B Absolutely. It seems to me that teenagers are becoming more violent because of TV.

C I don't know. I don't think people learn violent behavior from TV.

Give an opinion

If you ask me, . . .
It seems to me that . . .
I don't think . . .

Agree

Definitely.
Absolutely.
You're right.
That's for sure.

2 The way it used to be

Complete the story with the correct form of the verbs below.

| be | bring | buy | complain | get | hate | live | play | push | ✓visit |

When I was a kid, we used to _____visit_____ my grandparents every month. They _____ two hours from our home, so we always _____ some books to read in the car. I used to _____ the drive, and I'd always _____ , so my dad would _____ us ice cream. That _____ fun. When we _____ to my grandparents' house, my grandma would always let us _____ in her yard. They had a swing set, and my grandpa would _____ us on the swings.

3 How many words can you remember?

Write expressions with *do* or *make* about six family members or friends. Then tell a partner about each person, using the expressions.

1. my uncle George → makes his living as a teacher / doesn't make a lot of money

2. my friend Yoko → does medical research

"My uncle George makes his living as a teacher. He doesn't make a lot of money, but he loves his work."

4 *What's going to happen?*

Complete the conversation with appropriate ways to talk about the future, using the verbs given. More than one correct answer is possible in some cases. Then practice with a partner.

Cindy What time __does__ your train ____leave____ (leave) today?

Dana I _____ (take) the 3:30 train. Oh, no, it's almost 3:00!

Cindy Don't worry. I _____ (drive) you to the station.

Dana Oh, you don't have to do that. I _____ (call) a taxi.

Cindy No way! I can take you. I _____ (go) to the mall this afternoon. It's not far from the train station.

Dana Are you sure it _____ (not be) a problem?

Cindy No problem at all. I _____ (meet) a friend there at 4:00.

Dana Well, OK. Thanks. I _____ (get) my suitcase.

Cindy Yeah. We _____ (have to) leave right away.

Dana OK. I _____ (be) ready in five minutes.

5 *A healthy diet?*

A Complete the sentences with different foods. Use your own ideas. Then discuss with a partner. Do you agree?

1. It's not healthy to eat too many __hamburgers__ .
2. If you want to lose weight, eat very few _____ .
3. If you eat too much _____ , you'll gain weight.
4. You should drink very little _____ .
5. A little _____ every day is good for you.
6. People should eat less _____ and more _____ .

B *Pair work* Replace the underlined words in these sentences. How many true sentences can you make? Compare with a partner.

1. I like boiled eggs better than fried eggs.
2. I drink about three cans of soda.
3. I'm trying to eat less ice cream and fewer donuts.
4. I always keep a jar of mayonnaise in my refrigerator.
5. I ate too much candy and not enough fruit yesterday.

A I like roast chicken better than fried chicken. How about you?
B Actually, I prefer barbecued chicken.

6 *Get off the phone!*

Role play Student A: You are planning a special dinner for an English-speaking visitor to your country. Phone your partner to ask for advice about what kind of food to prepare.

Student B: Your partner calls to ask for advice just as you are leaving to meet a friend. Try to end the conversation politely.

Self-check

How sure are you about these areas? Circle the percentages.

grammar
20% 40% 60% 80% 100%
vocabulary
20% 40% 60% 80% 100%
conversation strategies
20% 40% 60% 80% 100%

· ·

Study plan

What do you want to review? Circle the lessons.

grammar
4A 4B 5A 5B 6A 6B
vocabulary
4A 4B 5A 5B 6A 6B
conversation strategies
4C 5C 6C

Relationships

In Unit 7, you learn how to . . .

- make sentences with subject and object relative clauses.
- use phrasal verbs like *grow up*, *get along*, and *break up*.
- talk about friendships, dating, and other relationships.
- soften comments with expressions like *I think*, *probably*, *kind of*, and *in a way*.
- use *though* to give a contrasting idea.

Before you begin . . .

How many different relationships do you have with other people? Are you a family member, a friend, a teacher, a student, a co-worker? Which relationship do you enjoy most?

Christopher Owen talks about his circle of friends.

2 My most exciting friend . . .

"Jennifer is another friend from college. Jen plays in a rock band that's really hot right now, so her life is very different from mine. She still calls a lot to talk about all the things she's doing. That's kind of fun."

1 My running buddy . . .

"Well, Mike is the guy I run with in the morning. He's the one who got me started running when I was in college. It's convenient because he lives right down the street."

3 My roommate . . .

"Toshiro is a guy that Jen introduced me to. He was looking for an apartment to share. It's great because he's a 'clean freak.' I've never lived in a place that's so clean."

6 My oldest friend . . .

"Charlie is someone I grew up with. We've been through a lot together. I can tell him just about anything. He's just someone I can totally trust."

5 A new friend . . .

"Then there's Angela. She's a new friend I met through Mike. She's cool. She's the kind of person you can just call and say, 'You want to go see a movie tonight?' That kind of thing."

4 A friend from work . . .

"Nina is an interesting woman who sits across from me at work. She used to have a company that planned weddings for people. She has some funny stories to tell."

1 Getting started

A Listen and read the article. How did Christopher meet his friends?

Figure it out ➔ **B** How does Christopher express these ideas? Underline the sentences in the article.

1. Jen plays in a rock band. It's really hot right now.
2. Nina is an interesting woman. She sits across from me at work.
3. Angela is a new friend. I met her through Mike.

66

2 Grammar   *Relative clauses*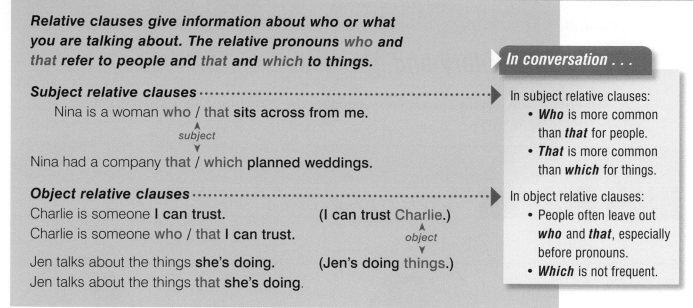

**Relative clauses give information about who or what
you are talking about. The relative pronouns who and
that refer to people and that and which to things.**

▶ **In conversation . . .**

Subject relative clauses · ▶

   Nina is a woman **who** / **that** sits across from me.
                    ▲
               subject
               ▼

   Nina had a company **that** / **which** planned weddings.

In subject relative clauses:
- ***Who*** is more common
  than ***that*** for people.
- ***That*** is more common
  than ***which*** for things.

Object relative clauses · ▶

Charlie is someone **I can trust.**   (I can trust Charlie.)
Charlie is someone **who** / **that** I can trust.   ▲
                                       object
                                       ▼

Jen talks about the things **she's doing.**   (Jen's doing things.)
Jen talks about the things **that** she's doing.

In object relative clauses:
- People often leave out
  who and ***that***, especially
  before pronouns.
- ***Which*** is not frequent.

A Combine each pair of sentences. Use relative clauses. More than one answer
may be possible.

1. I have a friend. She calls me a lot to talk about her problems.

   I have a friend who calls me a lot to talk about her problems. (I have a friend that . . .)

2. I made some new friends at a club. It organizes hiking trips and things like that.

   _____

3. My best friend has a guitar. She bought it from a rock star.

   _____

4. I know someone. He has a big party once a year for all his friends.

   _____

5. I have a really interesting friend. I met her at my health club.

   _____

6. I found this cool Web site. It helps you find your old school friends.

   _____

B **Pair work** Change the information above. Make true sentences. Tell a partner.

"I have a friend who calls me a lot to talk about his roommate."   *"Really? Are they having problems?"*

3 Talk about it   *Who's in your circle of friends?*

Group work Discuss the questions. Do you want to meet any of your classmates' friends?

▶ Who's your closest friend? How did you meet?
▶ Do you have any friends that you met through other friends?
▶ Do you keep in touch with any of the friends you grew up with?
▶ Do you have any friends who have exciting lives? Explain why.
▶ Do you have friends you chat with online? Where do they live?
▶ Do you have any friends who are very different from you? How are they different?

1 *Building vocabulary and grammar*

A 💿 Put the story in the correct order. Number the parts from 1 to 6. Then listen and check your answers.

High School *Sweethearts*

☐ He discovered that Anna was a member. He wrote her an e-mail, and she **wrote back** right away. It **turned out** that Anna was still single and was looking for him, too! They made plans to meet at a restaurant in her city.

☐ Steve and Anna **grew up** in a small town called Greenville. In high school, they **hung out** with the same crowd. They **got along** very well, and they started **going out** together. Anna was Steve's first love, and he was her first love, too.

☐ When Steve was 35, he was ready to **settle down** with someone, but no one seemed right. He still thought about Anna. Then he heard about a Web site that helps people find old classmates. He **signed up** immediately.

Anna and Steve at their high school prom

☐ But the long-distance relationship didn't **work out**, and they decided to **break up**. A year later, Anna's family **moved away** from Greenville, and Steve lost touch with her.

☐ When they saw each other, all the old memories **came back**, and they started **going out** again. Within a few months, they were married, and they are now living "happily ever after." Sometimes your first love **turns out** to be the best.

☐ After they graduated, Anna **went away** to college, while Steve attended a college nearby. They would get together about once a month, when Anna **flew back** home to visit her parents.

A recent photo of the happy couple

Figure it out

B Which verbs in the story mean the same as the underlined expressions below?

1. Steve and Anna <u>spent their childhood</u> in the same town.
2. Steve and Anna started <u>dating</u>.
3. Anna <u>went</u> to college <u>in a different city</u>.
4. Steve and Anna decided to <u>stop dating</u>.

Word sort

C Complete the chart with two-part verbs from the story. Can you use four of the verbs to retell Steve and Anna's story?

along	away	back	down	up	out
		write back			

2 Grammar *Phrasal verbs*

> **A phrasal verb is a verb plus a particle like along, away, back, out, up, etc.**
>
> Steve and Anna **grew up** in the same town.
> They **got along** well and started **going out** together.
> Anna **went away** to college.
> She **flew back** home once a month.
> Things didn't **work out**, so they decided to **break up**.
>
> **Notice:**
> Steve and Anna **got along** well.
> Steve **got along with** Anna.
> Anna **got along with** Steve.
>
> Steve and Anna **went out** together.
> Steve **went out with** Anna.
> Anna **went out with** Steve.

A Read these opinions about relationships. Complete the sentences with the phrasal verbs below.

break up	get along	go back	✓go out	settle down	sign up	work out

1. It's more fun to _go out_ with someone you know than to go on a "blind date."
2. If you don't _____ well with your boyfriend's or girlfriend's family, your relationship won't _____ .
3. It's good to date a lot of different people before you _____ with one person.
4. After you _____ with someone, you should try and stay friends.
5. You should never _____ to someone you've broken up with.
6. If you want to meet someone, it's a good idea to _____ for a class.

About you → **B** *Pair work* Discuss the opinions above. Do you agree?

3 Speaking naturally *Stress in phrasal verbs*

> Are you going/out with anyone?   How are you getting along?

A Listen and repeat the questions above. Notice that the particle is stressed more than the verb.

About you → **B** *Group work* Ask and answer the questions. How many different opinions do you have?

1. Do you think it's OK to go out with more than one person at the same time?
2. What should you do if you're not getting along with your boyfriend or girlfriend?
3. Do you think long-distance relationships can work out?
4. Is it OK to go out with someone who is a lot older or younger than you?
5. What's a good age to settle down?
6. What's the best way to break up with someone?

4 Vocabulary notebook *Matching up*

See page 74 for a new way to log and learn vocabulary.

They're probably just busy.

1 Conversation strategy *Softening comments*

A Which comment in each pair sounds "softer"?

1. *a. It's weird.*
   b. It's kind of weird.

2. *a. They sort of ignore me.*
   b. They ignore me.

3. *a. They're shy.*
   b. Maybe they're a little shy.

Now listen. What does Maria think about her new neighbors?

Maria	*That's the couple that moved in next door.*
Chen	*Yeah? They seem pretty friendly.*
Maria	*Yeah. It's kind of weird, though. Sometimes they say hello, and other times they sort of ignore me.*
Chen	*Maybe they're just a little shy.*
Maria	*Oh, I think they're probably just busy or stressed out.*
Chen	*Yeah. Well, who isn't these days?*
Maria	*Actually, the woman is a bit more friendly. I've spoken to her a few times. We only talked about the weather, though.*
Chen	*That's how most of the people are in my building. I guess that's OK in a way. I don't like to get too friendly with the neighbors.*
Maria	*Yeah, me either.*

Notice how Maria and Chen use these expressions to "soften" their comments. Find examples in the conversation.

I guess / I think	a little / a (little) bit
probably / maybe	just
kind of / sort of	in a way

B Add the expressions in parentheses to these comments to make them softer. Compare with a partner.

1. My neighbors are unfriendly. (a little bit) They think they're better than everybody else. (maybe)
2. The people next door go to bed early. (kind of) They get annoyed when I have parties. (sort of)
3. The people across the street are always looking out of their window. They seem nosy. (a little) They don't have anything better to do. (I guess)
4. The guy above me plays the drums too loud. (a bit) It gets noisy. (kind of)
5. One of my neighbors is always coming over. It's irritating. (in a way) She's lonely. (I think / probably / just)

About you → **C** *Pair work* Do you know anyone like the people above? Tell your partner about your neighbors or someone else you know. Can you "soften" your comments?

"My neighbors are nice, but their kids are a bit noisy."

SELF-STUDY
AUDIO CD
CD-ROM

2 Strategy plus *though*

You can use
though to
give a contrasting
idea.

They seem pretty friendly.

It's kind of weird, though. Sometimes they sort of ignore me.

A Match each comment with a response that gives a contrasting idea. Then practice with a partner.

In conversation . . .

Though is one of the top 200 words.

1. I always think it's nice to socialize with the people you work with. ____
2. I find I go out with friends almost every night. ____
3. I try not to get too friendly with my neighbors. ____
4. I enjoy making new friends all the time. ____
5. I spend most of my free time at home by myself. ____

a. It's good to spend some time at home, though.
b. You shouldn't forget about your old friends, though.
c. It's not a good idea to date someone from work, though.
d. It's important to get along with them, though.
e. It's not good to spend too much time alone, though.

B *Pair work* Are the comments above true for you? Do you agree with the responses?

3 Listening and speaking *People I look forward to seeing*

A Listen to Matthew talk about the three people below. What contrasting information does he give about each person? Complete the sentences.

❶ The woman in the coffee shop gets stressed out. She's very _____ , though.

❷ My Web-design teacher is really nice. He's kind of _____ , though.

❸ My yoga instructor is incredibly easygoing. He can be a bit _____ , though.

B Listen again. Why does Matthew look forward to seeing each person? Write a reason under each picture.

C *Pair work* Tell a partner about three people you enjoy seeing. Answer your partner's questions about them.

1 Reading

A Have you lost touch with anyone from your past? Who are they? What do you remember about them? Tell the class.

B Read the article. What does this Web site do?

Web site chaperones[1] classmate reunions

By Jefferson Graham, USA TODAY

When Ray Sears stumbled onto[2] the Classmates.com Web site, which promises to reunite old friends, he found a listing for his old seventh-grade girlfriend Gina, paid the membership fee so he could reconnect, and asked if she remembered him. "How could I forget my first love?" she replied.

Fast-forward to today, where the newly married Gina Sears is expected to give birth in August to Ray and Gina's first child.

"This is the promise of the Internet," says Sears, 32, a security supervisor at a Los Angeles-area shopping mall. "A simple way for the regular Joes[3] to find people from their past. It's a really neat way of getting back in touch."

Others apparently agree. The number of visitors to Classmates tripled in 2002, making it one of the most popular sites on the Web. It attracts 15 million visitors a month, and ranks No. 20 on Jupiter Media Metrix's list of top-traffic Web sites.

Making connections has been one of the most popular uses of the Internet, whether by e-mail, bulletin board, or instant messaging. But Classmates.com, like many online dating sites, has figured out a way to make people's need to connect pay off.

Classmates is a rare dot-com success story, a profitable company with two million paying subscribers who happily fork over[4] $36 a year (just increased from $30) to reach out to former classmates, military colleagues, even original birth parents.

How Classmates works: You go to the Web site and fill out forms with your schools, years attended, and other information. Then check the database – 180,000 U.S. schools and 38,000 military units – to see if old pals have also registered. You can see their names, but if you want to make contact, you must first become a paying member. The contacts are made through Classmates' private e-mail system – personal information isn't listed on the site.

Beyond listing schools, the military, and working the reunion markets, Classmates plans to launch a workplace version in the coming months to attract former co-workers who have since lost touch. The site also is looking to add an instant-messaging system so visitors can chat while they're on the site.

1 *chaperones*   supervises
2 *stumbled onto*   found by accident
3 *regular Joes*   ordinary people
4 *fork over*   pay

C Read the article again. Are the sentences true or false? Correct the false sentences.

	True	False
1. Gina didn't remember Ray Sears when he contacted her.	☐	☐
2. Gina and Ray are now married and starting a family.	☐	☐
3. Classmates.com helps you find old school friends.	☐	☐
4. You can contact your old friends for free.	☐	☐
5. The Web site doesn't give out your address and telephone number.	☐	☐

2 *Speaking and listening* *Getting back in touch*

About you →

A *Pair work* How do friends lose touch with each other? Add ideas to the list.
Have you ever lost touch with a friend? Tell your partner how it happened.

Friends lose touch when one of them . . .

- moves away.
- gets married.
- gets interested in different things.
- gets too busy with school or work.
- _____
- _____

B Listen to Javier talk about his friends. Does he want to get back in touch with them? Check (✓) the correct boxes.

	Yes	No	Don't know	Why did he lose touch?
1. *his college friends*	☐	☐	☐	_____
2. *his running buddy*	☐	☐	☐	_____
3. *his old girlfriend*	☐	☐	☐	_____

C Listen again. Why did Javier lose touch with his friends? Complete the rest of the chart.

3 *Writing* *Your circle of friends*

A Choose three friends. Write an article about them like the one on page 66. Include photos if you can.

Think about . . .

- how you met and why you became friends.
- what your friends are like.
- what you have in common.
- what you do together.

Document 1

My circle of friends

My best friend from high school

Ronaldo is a friend I met on my first day of high school. We sat next to each other in art class. Neither of us was very good at art, but we had a good time together in class. He's very easygoing. He's the kind of guy who gets along with everyone. We're both science-fiction fans, so we spend a lot of time at the movies.

> **Help note**
>
> **Both** and **neither**
>
> We're **both** science-fiction fans.
> **Both of us** are science-fiction fans.
>
> We **both** like going to the movies.
> **Both of us** like going to the movies.
>
> **Neither of us** was very good at art.

B *Pair work* Exchange articles with a partner. Ask questions about your partner's friends.

4 *Free talk* *What's important?*

See *Free talk 7* at the back of the book for more speaking practice.

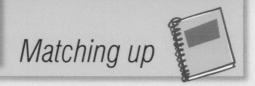

Matching up

Learning tip *Phrasal verbs*

When you learn a phrasal verb, it's a good idea to write down

- some other verbs you can use with the particle.

> <u>back</u>: get back / call back / fly back

- some other particles you can use with the verb.

> go: go back / go out / go away

Get away!

The most common verbs with the particles *away* and *back* are:

get	
go	
throw	⎤ away
put	⎦

go	
get	
come	⎤ back
call	⎦

1 Circle the two verbs in each list that go with the particle on the right.

1. go / move / hang   **away**
2. wake / eat / work   **out**
3. come / break / get   **back**
4. wake / go / come   **over**
5. sign / grow / sleep   **up**
6. fall / eat / settle   **down**

2 Complete each expression with a different verb.

wake		in the morning
		with your boyfriend / girlfriend
	up	for a class
		without an alarm clock
		in a small town

		with your friends
		late
	out	to a club
		at a nice restaurant
		at the gym

3 *Word builder* How many new phrasal verbs can you make from these particles?

away	*back*	*down*	*out*	*up*

On your own

Make a flip pad with headings for different topics such as "Relationships," "Going out," and "Daily routines." How many phrasal verbs can you write for each topic? Carry the flip pad with you, and learn the words whenever you have a moment.

Relationships
work out
get along
break up

What if?

In Unit 8, you learn how to . . .
- talk about imaginary situations or events in the present and future.
- talk about how you wish your life were different and why.
- discuss how to deal with everyday dilemmas.
- give advice using expressions like *If I were you* . . . and *You could* . . . .
- use *That would be* . . . to comment on a possibility or a suggestion.

Before you begin . . .
What are your priorities in life? Rank these things in order from 1 (most important) to 6 (least important).

☐ family	☐ career	☐ physical appearance
☐ friends	☐ wealth	☐ happiness

What other things matter to you?

How do you wish your LIFE were DIFFERENT?

" I just wish I weren't so busy with my work. I have to work most weekends, so I never have enough time to do anything fun. If I had more free time, I'd go kayaking every weekend. "

— *Berta Palmas, Monterrey*

" We just got married, and we're renting a tiny little apartment. It would be great if we could afford a bigger place to live. We don't have enough room for all our stuff. "

— *Min Sup and Jin Eun Cho, Seoul*

" Well, I never get to go away on holiday. I just don't have enough money. So, I wish I had enough money to go somewhere exciting. Yeah, if I could choose anywhere, I'd probably go to Egypt to see the pyramids. That would be great! "

— *Bryan Gibson, Melbourne*

" I wish I didn't live so far away from my family. My sister just had a baby — a little boy — and I never get to see him. I really miss everyone. If I lived closer, I'd be able to help out. "

— *Irene Chang, Taipei*

1 Getting started

A Listen to the people talk about their wishes. What do they want?

> **Figure it out**

B Are these sentences true or false? Find sentences above to support your answers.

1. Berta wants to go kayaking more often.
2. Min Sup and Jin Eun have enough money for a bigger place.
3. Bryan is going to Egypt this year.
4. Irene lives close to her sister.

2 Grammar Wishes and imaginary situations or events

Wishes for the present or future:	Imaginary situations or events in the present or future:
wish + past form of verb	**If + past form of verb . . . would (could) + verb**

I wish I **had** more free time.　　　　If I **had** more free time, I'**d** / I **would go** kayaking.
(I **don't have** enough free time,　→　so I **don't go** kayaking.)

I wish I **weren't** so busy with my work.　　If I **were** less busy, I **could go away** on the weekends.
(I'**m** very busy with my work,　→　so I **can't go away** on the weekends.)

We wish we **could afford** to move.　　If we **could afford** to move, we **wouldn't live** in this tiny place.
(We **can't afford** to move,　→　so we **live** in this tiny place.)

She wishes she **didn't live** so far away.　　If she **lived** closer, she'**d** / she **would be able to** help out.
(She **lives** very far away,　→　so she **isn't able to** help out.)

A Complete the sentences with the appropriate form of the verbs given, as in the example.

1. I wish I __had__ (have) more money. If I __earned__ (earn) more, I __could have__ (can have) my own apartment, and I __wouldn't have to__ (not have to) live with my parents.

2. I wish I _____ (not have to) commute three hours a day. If I _____ (can find) a job closer to home, then I _____ (not waste) so much time on the train.

3. I wish I _____ (can finish) my degree this year. If I _____ (have) a degree, then I _____ (can get) a job, and I _____ (be able to) pay off my student loans.

4. I wish I _____ (can do) something more exciting with my life. If I _____ (have) the chance, I _____ (work) in another country or something like that.

> **In conversation . . .**
>
> People say **I wish I was . . .** and **If I was . . .** more frequently than **I wish I were . . .** and **If I were . . .** , but this is not considered correct in written English.
>
> **I wish I was . . .**
>
> **I wish I were . . .**

About you → **B** *Pair work* Discuss the sentences above. Do you have any of these wishes?

"Well, I definitely wish I had more money. But I wouldn't look for my own apartment. I'd . . . "

3 Listening and speaking A wish for today

A Listen. What wishes do these people have for today? Number the topics they talk about.

☐ **social life**　　☐ **the weather**　　☐ **family**　　☐ **work**

_____　　_____　　_____　　_____

B Listen again. Why do they wish for these things? Write a reason under each topic.

About you → **C** *Group work* What's your wish for today? Tell the group. Do you have similar wishes?

Life's little dilemmas

1 Building vocabulary and grammar

A Listen and take the quiz. Circle your answers. Then compare with a partner.

What would you do?

1. What would you do if a friend broke your mother's favorite teapot? Would you . . .

   a. let your friend buy a new one?
   b. tell your friend not to **worry about** it and **buy** a new teapot **for** your mom?

2. What would you do if you **borrowed** a camera **from** a friend and broke it? Would you . . .

   a. simply **apologize for** breaking it?
   b. take it to a store and **pay for** the repairs?

3. How would you react if a friend started dating someone you used to go out with? Would you . . .

   a. **talk to** your friend **about** your feelings?
   b. feel hurt but **say** nothing **to** either of them?

4. What would you do if a friend came for dinner and brought an expensive box of chocolates? Would you . . .

   a. **thank** your friend **for** the gift and not open it?
   b. **share** the chocolates **with** your friend after dinner?

5. What would you say if a friend **asked** you **for** a loan to buy an MP3 player? Would you say . . . ?

   a. "Sorry, I never **lend** money **to** anyone."
   b. "I'll **think about** it and let you know."

6. What would you do if a friend borrowed a favorite CD and forgot to return it? Would you . . .

   a. **remind** your friend **about** it several times?
   b. **forget about** it and buy yourself a new one?

B *Pair work* Find the prepositions that go with the expressions below. Then take turns using each expression in a true sentence.

1. worry <u>about</u> something
2. talk to someone _____ something
3. think _____ something
4. remind someone _____ something
5. forget _____ something
6. buy something _____ someone
7. pay _____ something
8. apologize _____ doing something
9. thank someone _____ something
10. ask someone _____ something
11. borrow something _____ someone
12. say something _____ someone
13. lend something _____ someone
14. share something _____ someone

"Sometimes I worry about money."

C Can you make questions about imaginary situations? Circle the correct words. Then ask and answer the questions with a partner.

1. What **would you do** / **did you do** if your friend **would forget** / **forgot** your birthday?
2. How **did you react** / **would you react** if a friend **told** / **would tell** your secret to everyone?

2 *Speaking naturally* *Intonation in long questions*

How would you react if a friend started dating someone you used to go out with?

What would you do if a friend came for dinner and brought an expensive box of chocolates?

A Listen and repeat each part of the long questions above. Notice how the intonation falls and then rises in the first and second parts of the questions, and then falls at the end.

B *Pair work* Find a new partner, and take the quiz on page 78 again. Take turns asking the questions, paying attention to the intonation of the long questions.

3 *Grammar* *Asking about imaginary situations or events*

What **would** you **do if** you **broke** a friend's camera?   **Would** you **pay** for a new one?
   I'd **apologize** for breaking it.   Yes, I **would**. / No, I **wouldn't**.
   I'd **pay** for the repairs.
   I **wouldn't say** anything about it.

A Make questions with *would* using the ideas below. Compare with a partner.

1. you find a wallet on the sidewalk outside a school / leave it there

   What would you do if you found a wallet on the sidewalk outside a school? Would you leave it there?

2. you hear a scream in the street at night / go outside to see what happened

   _____

3. a salesperson forgets to charge you for something / tell him or her about it

   _____

4. you damage a car in a parking lot / leave a note with your name and number

   _____

5. you are half an hour late meeting a friend for dinner / expect him or her to wait for you

   _____

6. you break something in a store / offer to pay for it

   _____

B *Pair work* Take turns asking the questions above. Discuss your answers. Do you agree?

A What would you do if you saw a wallet on the sidewalk outside a school? Would you leave it there?
B Um, no. I think I'd probably take it to the school office. What would you do?

4 *Vocabulary notebook* *Imagine that!*

See page 84 for a new way to log and learn vocabulary.

1 Conversation strategy *Giving advice*

A What advice would you give in this situation? Complete the reply.

A *I got into two grad schools. I got a scholarship at one school, but I think the other one is better.*
B *Well, if I were you, I'd _____ .*

Now listen. What advice does Nicole give Carlos about grad school?

Nicole *Hey, I hear you got accepted to grad school.*

Carlos *Yeah. I got into MSU and Bracken Tech.*

Nicole *Congratulations! So, where are you going to go?*

Carlos *I don't know. I got a full scholarship to Bracken Tech, but I think MSU has a better engineering department.*

Nicole *Well, if I were you, I'd take the scholarship. Then you wouldn't have to borrow any money.*

Carlos *Yeah, that would be great. But it's a tough decision.*

Nicole *Well, Bracken Tech's a good school. I mean, you might want to go there and meet some of the professors.*

Carlos *That'd be good. But then, everybody I know is going to MSU.*

Nicole *Oh, I wouldn't worry about that. You can make new friends. And anyway, I might go to Bracken next year, you know, if I get accepted.*

Carlos *Really? That would be awesome!*

Notice how Nicole gives advice to Carlos. She uses expressions like these. Find examples in the conversation.

If I were you, I'd . . .	*You might want to . . .*
I would / I'd . . .	*You could . . .*
I wouldn't . . .	

B Think of some advice for each problem below. Compare ideas with a partner.

1. "One of my co-workers just got a promotion, but my boss didn't give me one."
2. "I wish I weren't majoring in history, because I really don't like it very much."
3. "My boss wants me to transfer to another city, but I'm not sure I want to go."
4. "I really don't know what to do when I graduate from college."
5. "My aunt gave me this sweater for a gift, but it's not my style. I'll never wear it."

"If I were you, I'd meet with your boss and . . ."

C *Pair work* Role-play two of the problems above. Take turns giving advice.

A *My boss wants me to transfer to another city, but I'm not sure I want to go.*
B *Yeah, that's a difficult decision. You might want to . . .*

SELF-STUDY
AUDIO CD
CD-ROM

2 Strategy plus *That would be . . .*

You can use
That would be . . . to comment on a possibility or a suggestion.

> You might want to go there and meet some of the professors.

> That'd be good.

> I might go to Bracken next year.

> Really? That would be awesome!

A Complete the conversations. Then practice with a partner.

1. *A* If you could do something really different, what would you do?
   B Well, I'd really like to go on an archaeological dig in Mexico.
   A Really? Wow! That would be _____ !

2. *A* If you could have any job, what would you do?
   B Something creative. I'd like to be a writer or a musician or something.
   A Yeah. That'd be _____ .

3. *A* If you could go anywhere on vacation, where would you go?
   B That's easy. I'd go on a safari in Africa.
   A Oh, that would be _____ .

4. *A* Would you ever like to get a PhD in something?
   B Yeah, maybe one day. But it's impossible right now. I have my job and the kids. I'd have to study at midnight!
   A Oh, yeah. That would be _____ .

> **In conversation . . .**
>
> The most frequent adjectives after ***That would be . . .*** are ***nice***, ***good***, ***great***, ***fun***, ***cool***, ***interesting***, ***fine***, ***wonderful***, ***neat***, ***hard***, and ***awesome***.

About you → **B** *Pair work* Ask and answer the questions, giving your own answers. Continue the conversations.

3 Speaking and listening *Here's my advice.*

A Read about Tom's dilemma. What advice would you give? Tell the class.

Tom works for a big international company. He has a great job that pays well, but he doesn't really get along with his co-workers.

B Listen to Tom's conversations with three friends, and complete the chart.

What is the advice?		Is it helpful?	
		Yes	**No**
1. Amy	_____	☐	☐
2. Sam	_____	☐	☐
3. Louisa	_____	☐	☐

C *Group work* Discuss the advice. Which advice is the most helpful? the least helpful? Why?

1 Reading

A Brainstorm! Think of three ideas to complete each sentence. Tell the class.

"If I had my life to live over, I'd . . ."   *"If I had my life to live over, I wouldn't . . ."*

B Read the paragraph. What can you guess about the writer?

If I had my life to live over, . . .

I'd dare to make more mistakes next time. I'd relax, I'd limber up. I would be sillier than I've been this trip. I would take fewer things seriously, take more chances, take more trips. I'd climb more mountains and swim more rivers. I would eat more ice cream and fewer beans. I would perhaps have more actual troubles, but I'd have fewer imaginary ones. You see, I'm one of those people who lived seriously, sanely, hour after hour, day after day. Oh, I've had my moments, and if I had to do it over again, I'd have more of them. I've been one of those persons who never goes anywhere without a thermometer, a hot-water bottle, a raincoat, and a parachute. If I had to do it again, I would travel lighter than this trip. If I had my life to live over, I would start going barefoot earlier in the spring, and stay that way later in the fall. I would go to more dances. I would ride more merry-go-rounds. I would pick more daisies.

This paragraph has been attributed to many different sources.

C Find these sentences. What do the underlined expressions mean in the context of this paragraph?

1. *I'd relax, I'd limber up.* This means that the writer would be more
   a. flexible.   b. careful.   c. serious.

2. *I would be sillier than I've been this trip.* The writer uses "this trip" to refer to
   a. this year.   b. this decade.   c. this life.

3. *I would . . . take more chances, . . .* This means that the writer would do more
   a. safe things.   b. risky things.   c. serious things.

4. *Oh, I've had my moments, . . .* This means that the writer sometimes has acted
   a. more slowly.   b. more freely.   c. more carefully.

5. *If I had to do it again, I would travel lighter than this trip.* The writer would
   a. travel less.   b. worry less.   c. weigh less.

6. *I would pick more daisies.* This is a way of saying that the writer would
   a. do more work.   b. enjoy life more.   c. be more careful.

2 Speaking and writing *What would you change?*

A If you had last year to live over again, what would you change? Think of answers to the questions, and make notes below.

Is there . . .

■ a person you'd spend more time with?

_____

■ something you'd take more seriously?

_____

■ something you'd spend more time doing?

_____

■ something you'd worry about less?

_____

■ something you'd spend less time doing?

_____

■ a sport or activity you'd try?

_____

■ a place you'd go more often?

_____

■ a subject you'd study?

_____

About you →

B *Pair work* Take turns. Tell your partner about some things you'd change.

"I'd spend more time with my family and less time online."

C Choose one or more ideas from your list above. Write an article about changes you would make.

```
○○○          Document 1          ⊖
```

Things I'd change

If I had last year to live over again, I would definitely get more exercise. I definitely wouldn't watch so much TV, and I'd probably work out more at the gym. I'd try to stop eating so many snacks, but I probably would not give up ice cream because it's my favorite snack! If I got more exercise and ate less junk food, I'd lose some weight. I'd probably feel much healthier, too.

> **Help note**
>
> *Adverbs of certainty in affirmative and negative statements*
>
> Notice the position of the adverbs.
> *I would **definitely** get more exercise.*
> *I'd **probably** work out more at the gym.*
>
> But:
> *I **definitely** wouldn't watch so much TV.*
> *I **probably** would not give up ice cream.*

D Read your classmates' articles. Does anyone want to change the same things as you?

3 Free talk *What would you do?*

See *Free talk 8* at the back of the book for more speaking practice.

Vocabulary notebook

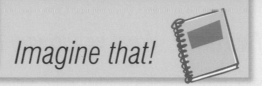

Imagine that!

Learning tip Verbs + prepositions

When you learn a new verb, find out what prepositions (if any) can come after it.
Remember that a verb coming after a verb + preposition has the form verb + *-ing*.

They <u>apologized for</u> making so much noise.

1 Read the problem below. Complete the possible solutions with the prepositions
about, *for*, and *to*.

You forget you have a dinner date with a friend, and you don't show up. Your friend calls
you, and she is very upset. What would you do?

1. I wouldn't worry _____ it. People usually forget _____ things like that.
2. I'd apologize immediately _____ forgetting _____ the date.
3. I'd offer to pay _____ dinner another time.
4. I'd tell her I was thinking _____ other things.
5. I wouldn't speak _____ her until she was less upset.
6. I'd blame my boss _____ keeping me in a meeting at work.
7. I'd wait _____ her to finish, and then I'd remind her _____
    the time she didn't meet me.

2 *Word builder* Find the prepositions that go with the verbs in the first column.
Then complete the sentences in the second column.

1. agree _____ someone _____ something	I agreed _____ my boss _____ the best solution.
2. apply _____ a job	He applied _____ a job with a software company.
3. explain something _____ someone	I explained the problem _____ my boss.
4. forgive someone _____ doing something	I forgave my friend _____ losing my CD.
5. invite someone _____ a party	My neighbor invited me _____ a party last week.
6. complain _____ someone _____ something	We complained _____ the neighbors _____ the noise.
7. blame someone _____ doing something	My parents blamed me _____ damaging their car.

On your own

Write 6 rules for living, using verbs
that take prepositions.

My rules for living
1. Never blame other
people for your problems.
2. Always forgive your

Tech savvy?

In Unit 9, you learn how to . . .

- include questions within questions and statements.
- use separable phrasal verbs like *turn on*, *plug in*, and *throw away*.
- use *how to* + verb, *where to* + verb, etc.
- talk about problems with technology and how things work.
- give different opinions with expressions like *Don't you think . . . ?*
- use *You know what I mean?* to ask someone to agree.

Before you begin . . .

How tech savvy are you? What electronic gadgets do you use in your everyday life? Do you ever have technical problems? Can you fix them?

Tech support

Nela
I have no idea why it's doing that.

Stephen
Have you checked the battery? Do you know if it's charged?

Hector
It's probably a software problem. We should call Yaman. Can anyone remember what Yaman's number is?

Kenji
There's something wrong with my computer. It keeps freezing up. Does anyone know what the problem is?

Tracy
The last time I had a computer problem, I went online for tech support. But I can't remember which Web site I used.

Jennifer
I wonder if you have that awful virus that's going around. Run your antivirus software.

Omar
I know what we should do. We should all have another cup of coffee.

Anita
You know what you should do? You should delete all your temporary Internet files. I forget how you do that, though.

Getting started

A 🔊 Listen. Kenji has a problem with his computer, but he doesn't know how to fix it. What solutions do his friends suggest?

Figure it out

B How do Kenji and his friends say the things below? Underline the sentences above. Compare with a partner.

1. What's the problem? Does anyone know?
2. Which Web site did I use? I can't remember.
3. How do you do that? I forget.
4. Maybe you have that awful virus.

2 Grammar *Questions within sentences*

Direct questions	Questions within questions	Questions within statements
What's the problem?	Do you know **what the problem is**?	I don't know **what the problem is**.
Which site did you use?	Can you remember **which site you used**?	I have no idea **which site I used**.
What should we do?	Do you know **what we should do**?	I know **what we should do**.
Why is it doing that?	Do you have any idea **why it's doing that**?	I have no idea **why it's doing that**.
Is the battery charged?	Do you know **if* the battery is** charged?	I wonder **if* the battery is charged**.

Use **if for **yes-no** questions.*

Notice the word order: What is the problem?

Do you know what **the problem is**?

> **In conversation . . .**
>
> *I don't know* is the most common three-word expression. *I don't know if* is the most common four-word expression.

A Rewrite these questions. Start with the expressions given.

1. How much does it cost to download music files off the Internet? (Do you know . . . ?)

    Do you know how much it costs to download music files off the Internet?

2. Are there any Internet cafés around here? (I wonder . . .)

    _____

3. Where can I buy a really cheap computer? (Do you know . . . ?)

    _____

4. How much did your cell phone cost? (Can you remember . . . ?)

    _____

5. How can I put my vacation photos on the Web? (Do you have any idea . . . ?)

    _____

6. How many songs can you store on an MP3 player? (I wonder . . .)

    _____

About you

B Group work Take turns asking your group the questions. Discuss the answers.

*A **Do you know how much it costs to download music files off the Internet?***
*B **I have no idea how much it costs. But it's probably not expensive.***
*C **I downloaded some songs once, but I don't remember how much I paid.***

3 Speaking and listening *What do you know about the Internet?*

A **Group work** Discuss the questions. Then listen and write the answers you hear.

1. Do you have any idea what percent of e-mail is spam? _____
2. Do you know what the biggest search engine is? _____
3. Do you know what the three most common languages on the Internet are? _____
4. Can you guess which continent has the most Internet users? _____
5. Can you guess how long the average Internet user spends online each week? _____

B Listen again. Write one more piece of information about the answer to each question.

1 Building language

A  Listen. What problem is Ken having? Practice the conversation.

Ken Pedro, how do you turn on the DVD player? I read the instruction manual, but I can't figure out how to do it.

Pedro Let's see. I think you can use the remote to turn it on. Do you know where it is?

Ken Yeah, it's right here.

Pedro OK, so let me show you what to do. First, you press this button. That turns the DVD player on. Huh. It's not working.

Ken I wonder if there's something wrong with the remote.

Pedro Actually, the problem is the DVD player. We need to plug it in!

Ken Oh, right.

Figure it out → **B** Circle the two correct choices in each question. Compare with a partner.

1. Do you **turn your TV on** / **turn on your TV** / **your TV turn on** every morning?
2. Do you **turn the TV off** / **turn it off** / **turn off it** when you're not watching it?
3. Do you know **to play** / **how to play** / **how you play** a DVD on a computer?

2 Grammar *Separable phrasal verbs; how to, where to, what to*

Separable phrasal verbs with objects	Examples:	Question word + *to* + verb
How do you — **turn on** the DVD player? **turn** the DVD player **on**? **turn** it **on**? (NOT ~~turn on it~~?)	plug in turn on turn off turn up turn down	Let me show you **what to do**. Can you show me **how to turn** it **on**? Do you know **where to plug** it **in**?

Complete the sentences as in the example. Then practice with a partner.

1. *A* Do you know how <u>to turn off this cell phone / to turn this cell phone off</u> ? (this cell phone / turn off)
   B This button <u>turns it off</u> . You need to push it really hard.

2. *A* I don't know how _____ . (the air conditioning / turn down)
   B I can show you how _____ . Just turn this dial.

3. *A* Can you show me where _____ ? (my laptop / plug in)
   B You can _____ right over there.

4. *A* I can't figure out how _____ . (the CD player / turn on)
   B I'm not sure how _____ . Maybe you press this button.

5. *A* Can you show me how _____ on my computer? (the volume / turn up)
   B I'm sorry, but I have no idea how _____ .

3 *Speaking naturally* Linking consonants and vowels

I'm not sure how to turn_it_on.   I don't know where to plug_it_in.

Listen and repeat the sentences above. Notice how the consonants are linked to the vowels. Then practice the questions and answers in Exercise 2 on page 88 again, this time with a new partner.

4 Building vocabulary

A Match the pictures with the sentences. Then work with a partner. Say what's happening in each picture.

"He's hooking up a computer."

a. Put them away.
b. Hook it up.
c. Look it up.
d. Pick it up.
e. Put it down.
f. Print it out.
g. Put them on.
h. Take them off.
i. Take it apart.
j. Throw it away.
k. Turn it down.
l. Turn it up.

Word sort ➤ **B** Make word webs using the expressions above and your own ideas. Then compare with a partner.

a computer

a radio

About you ➤ **C** *Group work* Ask and answer the questions.

1. What's the first thing you turn on in the morning? What else do you turn on?
2. What do you turn off at night before you go to bed?
3. What different things do you plug in during the day?
4. Do you always turn your cell phone off before class starts? Where else do you turn it off?

5 *Vocabulary notebook* On and off

See page 94 for a new way to log and learn vocabulary.

I know what you mean, but . . .

1 Conversation strategy *Giving different opinions*

A Read the conversation. Which response gives a different opinion? Check (✓) the box.

> *A* *I think chat rooms are a waste of time.*
>
> *B* ☐ *I know what you mean. They can be fun, though.*
>
>   ☐ *Yeah. I know what you mean.*

Now listen. What does Jacob think about Internet chat rooms? What about Greg?

Jacob **Are you on the Internet again?**

Greg **Yeah. I'm in a great chat room. It's a cool way to meet people.**

Jacob **I don't know. You don't really know who you're talking to. I mean, it's not like talking to someone in person. You know?**

Greg **That's true. You can still talk about interesting stuff, though. You know what I mean?**

Jacob **Well, I'm not sure. Don't you think it's more fun to talk to people, you know, face-to-face?**

Greg **I know what you mean, but it's not so easy to find people with the same interests.**

Jacob **Well, maybe. On the other hand, if you spent less time in chat rooms, you might find there are some interesting people around here. You know what I'm saying?**

Notice how Jacob and Greg give different opinions. They use expressions like these. Find examples in the conversation.

> *I know what you mean, but . . .*
> *That's true. (You) . . . , though.*
> *Maybe. On the other hand, . . .*
> *I don't know. / I'm not (so) sure. Don't you think . . . ?*

B *Pair work* Can you respond to each comment by giving a different opinion? Take turns making comments and responding. Can you continue the discussion?

1. *A* I love my new laptop. Now I can work at home on the weekends.
   B I don't know. Don't you think _____ ?

2. *A* I'll never get a cell phone. I don't want to get calls all the time.
   B I know what you mean, but _____ .

3. *A* Surfing the Internet is a big waste of time.
   B Maybe. On the other hand, _____ .

4. *A* E-mail is great for keeping in touch with friends and family.
   B That's true. _____ , though.

SELF-STUDY
AUDIO CD
CD-ROM

2 Strategy plus *You know what I mean?*

When you want someone to agree with you, you can use expressions like these.

You know what I mean?
You know?
You know what I'm saying?

You can still talk about interesting stuff, though. You know what I mean?

You know what I mean? is the most common five-word expression. It is five times more frequent than **You know what I'm saying?**, which is the seventh most common five-word expression.

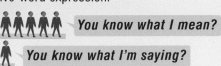

You know what I mean?

You know what I'm saying?

Pair work Complete each opinion below. Take turns presenting your ideas and responding.

1. "It seems to me people spend too much time on their computers. I mean,
   _____ . You know what I'm saying?"

2. "I don't think people should listen to music while they're working.
   _____ . You know?"

3. "I don't think you should go out with someone you meet on the Internet.
   _____ . You know what I mean?"

A *It seems to me people spend too much time on their computers. I mean, people*
   should spend more time with family and friends. You know what I'm saying?
B *I'm not sure. . . .*

3 Listening and speaking *The problem with technology*

A Listen to Hugo and Fran talking in a café. Who expresses these opinions? Check (✓) the boxes.

	Hugo	Fran
1. New technology is great. You can choose when and where to work.	☐	☐
2. New technology can make people work too much.	☐	☐
3. It's rude to talk to a friend on a cell phone when you're with another friend.	☐	☐
4. People shouldn't use their cell phones in places like cafés.	☐	☐
5. People should be able to use their cell phones wherever they are.	☐	☐

B Listen again to two of Hugo's opinions. Do you agree or disagree? Write responses. Then discuss with a partner.

1. _____   2. _____

1 Reading

A What types of personal information do you use to identify yourself? Complete the chart. When do you use this information? Who do you give it to?

General information	Numbers	Documents	Other
full name	bank account number	driver's license	passwords
home address			

B Read the magazine article. What do identity thieves do?

Robbing You **Blind**?

by Carla Fried
Real Simple Magazine

Thieves used to pick pockets and snatch handbags. Now they steal identities. . . . Identity thieves pilfer credit card information, bank statements, and national identification numbers so they can steal from existing accounts, open new ones, or even build up a criminal record under your name.

If you're lucky, you'll catch an ID thief while the stakes are still small – a couple of unauthorized purchases on a single credit card, say. If not, you'll discover you're a victim only when, for instance, a credit check shows overdue payments on dozens of credit cards you never even knew you had. . . . Here's how you can protect yourself where you are most vulnerable – mail, phone, and ATM – and avoid becoming the next statistic.

Identity theft often goes undetected until the damage has been done. Use these self-defense strategies to stop the crime before it starts.

Strategies for Stopping ID Thieves

Mail

DON'T:
■ **Have new blank checks sent to your mailbox.** Pick them up in person.
DO:
■ **Check monthly bills and statements for suspicious charges.** If you aren't getting a bill, this may be a sign that someone has stolen your account and had the billing address changed so you wouldn't notice their unauthorized charges.
■ **Shred personal documents before you throw them in the garbage.** Identity thieves rifle through garbage looking for discarded bills, bank statements, credit card receipts, and anything else that might contain information that could help them access your accounts or open a new one.

Phone

DON'T:
■ **Conduct sensitive business on your cell phone in public.** It's bad etiquette, and it can be a costly mistake if an identity thief is standing nearby and hears you give out some important personal information. (As long as your phone is a digital model, there is little chance of the signal being intercepted.)
DO:
■ **Protect the calling card you use to make long-distance calls from public phones.** It's best not to carry your card at all, but if you need to pull it out, watch out for "shoulder surfers" who could sell your calling card number or use it themselves. Some thieves use binoculars and telescopes to spy on victims in crowded areas.

ATM

DON'T:
■ **Use ATMs located in convenience stores.** They may not have the same security protection as bank ATMs.
DO:
■ **Use a PIN (Personal Identification Number) that's ridiculously hard to crack.** Don't use your birth date or phone number.
■ **Keep an eye out for shoulder surfers.** (See Phone, left.)

C Can you find words and expressions in the article with the following meanings?

1. steal _____
2. without permission _____
3. someone who has been robbed _____
4. in danger _____

5. cut in very small pieces _____
6. search quickly _____
7. figure out _____
8. watch out for _____

D Answer the questions. Then compare ideas with a partner.

1. What should you do when you want to throw away your credit card statements?
2. Why do identity thieves go through people's garbage?
3. Why is it a bad idea to call your bank from your cell phone when you're in a public place?
4. What do shoulder surfers do?
5. Why shouldn't you use your birth date as your PIN?

2 Speaking and writing *Keeping it safe*

A *Group work* Brainstorm ideas on how to make your personal information safe. Discuss the questions and take notes.

1. Would you let a friend or family member use your credit card?
2. Where should you keep your bank statements and credit card receipts?
3. What's the best way to remember your PIN?
4. Who would you give your PIN to?
5. Where's the safest place to keep your passport and other ID?
6. Do you have copies of your important documents?

A I would never let anyone use my credit card. It's just not safe. You know what I mean?
B Yeah, I know. I wouldn't let anyone use my phone card, either.

B Choose the best ideas to write a short article.

○○○   **Document 1**

Here are some dos and don'ts for keeping your personal information safe.

Credit cards
Do shred credit card bills. If you don't, a thief may find your credit card number in the garbage.

Don't give your credit card number to someone who calls you on the phone. Only give out your number if you have made the call and you trust the person you are talking to.

▶ **Help note**

Planning your article
- Write all your ideas down in any order. Don't worry about spelling and grammar.
- Choose the best ideas you want to use.
- Number your ideas to help you plan your article.
- Write the article.
- Check your spelling and grammar.

C Read your classmates' articles. Did you pick up any good tips from them?

3 Free talk *Tech trivia*

See *Free talk 9* for more speaking practice.

On and off

Learning tip *Writing short conversations*

When you learn expressions with a new or complex structure, think of everyday situations where you might use them. Write short conversations using the expressions.

The top 6 things people talk about *turning on* and *off* are their:

1. radio   4. phone
2. light(s)   5. computer
3. music   6. television

1 Complete the conversations. Use the sentences in the box.

I'll look it up.	✓ I'll turn it down.	Then I'd take them off.
I'll print it out.	I'll turn it up.	You can put them away in the closet.

1. *A* The music's too loud.

   B __I'll turn it down.__

2. *A* I don't know what to do with these boxes.

   B _____

3. *A* What does this word mean?

   B _____

4. *A* I need a copy of that document.

   B _____

5. *A* I can't hear the radio.

   B _____

6. *A* I'm allergic to these earrings.

   B _____

2 *Word builder* Find the meaning of the phrasal verbs in the sentences below. Think of a situation for each one, and complete the conversations.

1. *A* _____

   B Sure. What time should I **pick** you **up**?

2. *A* _____

   B It's a nice color. Why don't you **try** it **on**?

3. *A* _____

   B If you have the receipt, **take** it **back** to the store.

4. *A* _____

   B Actually, I'm late for work. Can I **call** you **back** tonight?

5. *A* _____

   B OK. I'd better **take** it **out** right now.

6. *A* _____

   B I'll show you how to **put** it **together**.

On your own

Make labels with different expressions to put around the house. When you have learned the expression, you can throw the label away.

Take it out.

1 How many words can you remember?

A How many different phrasal verbs can you use to complete the sentences below?

What can you say about relationships?		What can you do to a television?
You can	get along _____ _____	with someone.	You can	turn it on. _____ _____

B *Pair work* Compare with a partner. Score 1 point for each correct sentence. Score 2 points for a correct sentence your partner doesn't have.

2 Can you use these expressions?

Complete the conversation with the expressions in the box. Use capital letters where necessary. Then practice with a partner.

you might want to	✓ I know what you mean	don't you think	sort of
on the other hand	you know what I mean	I'm not so sure	though

Jan My boyfriend's phone is always busy. It drives me crazy.

Rob Oh, <u>I know what you mean</u> . My girlfriend never answers her cell phone.

Jan That's annoying. If you have a phone, you should always answer it.

Rob _____ . Sometimes it's _____ rude to answer the phone – if you're having dinner or something. _____ ?

Jan Yeah, but you can always answer and just say, "Can I call you back?" That's OK, _____ ?

Rob Maybe. _____ , if you don't answer it, the person can leave a message.

Jan Oh, no. I can't believe this. He's still on the phone.

Rob Well, _____ leave him a message.

Jan Yeah, I could do that. He never checks his voice mail, _____ .

3 Here's my problem. Any thoughts?

Write a piece of advice for each person below. Then role-play conversations in groups.

1. "My best friend doesn't study enough because he spends too much time on the Internet."
2. "I wish I could e-mail my parents, but they don't know how to use their computer!"
3. "My boyfriend / girlfriend wants to get married, but I'm not ready to settle down."
4. "I wish I had more money for travel. If I did, I could go to some pretty exciting places."

A **My best friend doesn't study enough because he spends too much time on the Internet.**

B **Well, you might want to talk to him about it.**

C **I don't know. If I were you, I wouldn't say anything to him. But you could . . .**

95

4 *I wish, I wish . . .*

A What do these people wish for and why? Complete the sentences. Compare with a partner.

1. I wish I __had__ (have) a car. If I __had__ (have) a car, I __could go__ (can go) places on the weekends.
2. I wish I _____ (know) how to swim. If I _____ (can swim), I _____ (be able to) go snorkeling with my friends.
3. I wish I _____ (can speak) Portuguese fluently. If I _____ (be) fluent, it _____ (be) easier to travel around Brazil.
4. I wish I _____ (have) more money. If I _____ (find) a part-time job, I _____ (earn) more money. On the other hand, I _____ (not have) enough time to study.
5. I wish I _____ (not have to) work tonight. If I _____ (be) free, I _____ (go out) with my friends.
6. I wish I _____ (know) how to use more software programs so I _____ (can get) a better job.

B *Pair work* Use the ideas above to tell a partner two things you wish. Explain why.

"I wish I had a motorcycle. If I had a motorcycle, I could ride it to work."

5 *I wonder . . .*

A Rewrite these questions about the picture. Compare with a partner.

1. What is it?   Do you know __what it is__ ?
2. How do you turn it on?   Can you tell me _____ ?
3. Does it still work?   I wonder _____ ?
4. How much did it cost?   Do you know _____ ?
5. How do you use it?   Can you tell me _____ ?

B *Pair work* Look at the picture, and ask and answer your questions.

A *Do you know what it is?*
B *Yes, it's an old record player.* **or** *I have no idea what it is.*

6 *It's all relative.*

A How many ways can you complete these questions? Use *who, that, which,* or no relative pronoun.

1. What do you do with electronic gadgets _____ don't work anymore?
2. What would you do if you got a gift _____ you didn't like?
3. What do you do when you see a word _____ you don't know?
4. What do you do with clothes _____ are out of style?
5. What would you do if you had neighbors _____ played their music too loud?

B *Pair work* Ask and answer the questions. Can you use a phrasal verb in your answers?

Self-check

How sure are you about these areas? Circle the percentages.

grammar
20% 40% 60% 80% 100%

vocabulary
20% 40% 60% 80% 100%

conversation strategies
20% 40% 60% 80% 100%

· ·

Study plan

What do you want to review? Circle the lessons.

grammar
7A 7B 8A 8B 9A 9B

vocabulary
7A 7B 8A 8B 9A 9B

conversation strategies
7C 8C 9C

What's up?

In Unit 10, you learn how to . . .

- use the present perfect continuous to talk about recent activities.
- use *since*, *for*, and *in* with the present perfect and present perfect continuous.
- use *already*, *still*, and *yet* with the present perfect.
- talk about your social life and different kinds of movies.
- ask someone for a favor politely.
- use *All right* and *OK* to move a conversation to a new topic.

Before you begin . . .

What's happening in your life these days? Have you . . .

- done anything special?
- been out with your friends?
- had a party?
- gone dancing anywhere?

- eaten anywhere nice?
- seen any good movies?
- been to any concerts?
- joined any clubs?

Bob So, what have you been doing since I saw you last?

Lois Working. That's pretty much it. I haven't been out in months. What about you?

Bob Same here. I've been working late every night. Uh . . . do you have time to grab a bite to eat?

Maya I haven't seen you in ages! What have you been up to?

Gail Well, you won't believe it, but I've been seeing a guy from work. We've gone out three or four times now, so I guess it's getting serious.

Will What have you been up to recently? I haven't seen you at the gym.

Diane Well, I've been going to a pottery class since September.

Will Pottery . . . really! So, what kind of things do you make?

Diane So far I've made eight vases and two bowls. Here's something I just made.

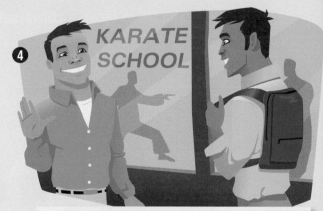

Juan Hey, good to see you. I see you're still doing karate.

Ahmad Oh, yeah.

Juan How long have you been doing that? About three years?

Ahmad Actually, for nine years now.

Juan Wow! That's impressive.

1 Getting started

A Listen. Who has some news to tell? Who doesn't?

Figure it out **B** Complete these sentences. Are any of them true for you? Tell a partner.

1. I've been _____ hard recently, so I haven't been out much.
2. I've _____ going out a lot with some friends from school.
3. I've been taking evening classes _____ a few years now.
4. I've known my best friend _____ I was in high school.
5. I haven't seen some of my friends _____ ages.

2 Grammar *Present perfect continuous vs. present perfect*

Use the present perfect continuous for an ongoing or repeated activity that started before now and continues into the present.	**Use the present perfect to show the results of an activity or how many times it has happened.**

What **have** you **been doing** lately?
  I'**ve been going** to a pottery class.   ➤

What things **have** you **made** so far?
  I'**ve made** eight vases and two bowls.

Who **has** she **been seeing**?
  She'**s been seeing** a guy from work.   ➤

How many times **have** they **gone out** together?
  They'**ve been** out three or four times.

Since, for, and in for duration
Use since with points in time. Use for and in with periods of time, but use in only in negative statements.

What have you been doing **since** I saw you last?
  Not much. I haven't been out **in** months, not **since** July.
How long has he been doing karate?
  He's been doing it **for** nine years.

▶ **In conversation . . .**

The present perfect is about 10 times more frequent than the present perfect continuous.

present perfect

present perfect continuous

A *Pair work* Ask and answer the questions. Continue your conversations.

Have you been . . .

1. eating out a lot recently?
2. listening to any good music lately?
3. spending a lot of time on the Internet?
4. going anywhere interesting on the weekends?
5. spending much time with your family lately?
6. getting any exercise recently?

A **Have you been eating out a lot recently?**

B **Actually, yeah. I've been eating out almost every night.**

A **Really? I haven't eaten out in ages. So, where have you been going?**

B *Pair work* Ask your partner the questions, and ask follow-up questions with *How long?* Then change roles.

1. Do you play any sports?
2. How well do you speak English?
3. Where did you meet your best friend?
4. Do you have any hobbies?
5. What neighborhood do you live in?
6. Are you a member of any clubs?

A **Do you play any sports?**

B **Yeah, sure. Basketball and soccer.**

A **How long have you been playing basketball?**

3 Speaking naturally *Reduction of have*

*What **have** you been doing for fun lately?*	*(What've)*
*How many times **have** you gone out this month?*	*(times've)*
*Where **have** you been hanging out?*	*(Where've)*

Listen and repeat the questions above. Practice the reduction of *have* to *'ve.*
Then ask and answer the questions. Continue your conversations.

1 Building vocabulary

A What kinds of movies are these? Label the pictures with the words in the box.
Can you think of other kinds of movies? Which ones do you like best?

❶ _____

❷ _____

❸ _____

❹ _____

❺ _____

❻ _____

❼ _____

❽ _____

> an action movie
> an animated film
> a horror movie
> a musical
> a (romantic) comedy
> a science-fiction movie
> a thriller
> a war movie

B 💿 What kind of movie is each person talking about? Complete the descriptions
with a type of movie. Then listen and check your answers.

❶ It's a _____ . **It's about** these two people who **fall in love** over the Internet. It's a great **love story**, and it's **funny**, too.

❷ It's a new _____ **set in** ancient China. Michelle Yeoh is in it. The **stunts** and the kung-fu **fight scenes** are amazing. It's kind of **violent**, though.

❸ I just saw this _____ . A family moves into an old house, and they find a **monster** living in the attic. It was so **scary** that I couldn't watch most of it.

❹ It's a _____ that **takes place** in Delhi. So it's in Hindi, but it's **subtitled**. The **costumes**, the dancing, and the music are just wonderful.

❺ It's a _____ . Matt Damon **plays** a spy who can't remember who he is. It was so exciting. I couldn't stand the **suspense**.

❻ It's about **aliens** who come to take over the Earth. It's a classic _____ . The **special effects** are incredible.

❼ I saw this _____ about two soldiers who are brothers. It's a **true story** with a really **sad ending**. I cried a lot. It's a real **tearjerker**.

❽ We saw this **hilarious** movie. It's one of those _____ for both kids and adults. Eddie Murphy is the voice of one of the **cartoon characters**.

> **Word
> sort**

C Make a word web about a movie you have seen. Then describe it to a partner.

It's a _____ .

It's about _____ .

_____ is in it.

It's set in _____ .

movie: _____

He / She plays _____ .

It takes place in _____ .

It _____ .

I _____ .

2 Building language

A Listen. What do Carl and Jolene decide to do? Why? Practice the conversation.

Carl Sorry I'm late. Have you been waiting long?

Jolene No, just a few minutes.

Carl So, which movie do you want to see? I've heard good things about *Starship*. Have you seen it yet?

Jolene Yeah. I've already seen it. It was OK.

Carl Oh. Well, there's *Funny Guy*. It's been playing for ages, and I still haven't seen it.

Jolene Actually, I saw it when it first came out.

Carl OK, well, how about *Joker*? I haven't seen that yet, either.

Jolene I've seen it, but I'll go again. It was hilarious. At the end, the guy falls into a . . .

Carl Hey, don't spoil it for me. Let's just go see it.

Figure it out → **B** Choose the correct word, and then complete each sentence with the name of a movie. Compare with a partner.

1. I **already / still / yet** haven't seen _____ .
2. I haven't seen _____ **already / still / yet**.
3. I've **already / still / yet** seen _____ .

3 Grammar *already, still, and yet with present perfect* 💿

Have you seen *Funny Guy* **yet**?	=	*I imagine you're planning to see it.*
Yes, I've **already** seen it. / Yes, I've seen it **already**.	=	*I saw it earlier.*
No, I haven't seen it **yet**. / No, not **yet**.	=	*I haven't seen it, but I plan to.*
No, I **still** haven't seen it.	=	*I've wanted to see it for weeks, but I haven't yet.*

A Complete the conversations. Add *already*, *still*, or *yet*. Then practice with a partner.

In conversation . . .

With this meaning of **yet**, about 83% of its uses are in negative statements and about 17% are in questions.

1. *A* There's a new Jackie Chan movie out. Have you seen it _____ ?

   B Yeah, I've _____ seen it. How about you?

   A No, not _____ . Actually, I _____ haven't seen his last one.

2. *A* Have you been to that new multiplex theater _____ ?

   B No. I really want to go, but I haven't had a chance _____ .

3. *A* Have you ever bought movie tickets online?

   B No, I _____ haven't signed up for Internet service. But I really should.

About you → **B** *Pair work* Start conversations like the ones above, changing the underlined words. Use your own information.

4 Vocabulary notebook *Great movies*

See page 106 for a new way to log and learn vocabulary.

I was wondering . . .

1 Conversation strategy *Asking for a favor politely*

A Can you choose the appropriate ways of asking your teacher or boss for a favor?

☐ *I want to leave early today.*
☐ *I was wondering if I could leave early today.*

☐ *Would it be OK if I left early today?*
☐ *I'm going to leave early today, OK?*

Now listen. What is Todd asking his boss, Paula, for?

Todd	**Excuse me. I was wondering if I could talk to you for a second.**
Paula	**Sure. Let me just send this e-mail. All right. So, what can I do for you?**
Todd	**Well, I wanted to ask a favor, actually.**
Paula	**OK.**
Todd	**I was wondering, would it be all right with you if I took Friday off?**
Paula	**This Friday?**
Todd	**Yes. I'm going away for the weekend, and, um, the traffic is always bad on Friday afternoons. So, I was thinking, if I took the day off, I could get an early start. Would that be OK with you?**
Paula	**Well, all right. As long as you finish everything before you go.**
Todd	**Oh, thanks. I definitely will.**
Paula	**OK. So, was that all? All right, well, have a good weekend.**

Notice the expressions Todd uses to ask for a favor politely. These expressions are useful in formal situations or if you are asking someone for a big favor. Find examples in the conversation.

I was wondering, . . .
I was wondering if I / you could . . .
I wanted to . . .
Would it be all right / OK with you if I (took, went, etc.) . . . ?

B *Pair work* Choose one of the situations below. Take turns playing the roles. Ask politely for each favor on the list.

Situation 1: At school or college
Student A: You are the teacher.
Student B: You are a student. You want to . . .
■ ask for help with some homework.
■ miss the next class to go to an interview.
■ ask for an extension on a paper.

Situation 2: At work
Student A: You are the boss.
Student B: You are an employee. You want to . . .
■ take next week off to go to a family reunion.
■ ask for more time to write a report.
■ borrow a laptop computer overnight.

SELF-STUDY
AUDIO CD
CD-ROM

2 *Strategy plus* *All right and OK*

You can use **All right** and **OK** to move a conversation to a new phase or topic.

All right. So, what can I do for you?

You can also use **All right** and **OK** to agree to requests.

Would that be OK with you?

Well, all right.

Listen to the conversation. How do the speakers use *all right* and *OK*? Write *A* if the speaker is <u>a</u>greeing and *M* if the speaker is <u>m</u>oving the conversation along. Then practice the conversation.

A I was wondering, do you have a minute to talk?
B All right. _A_ I'm free right now.
A Great. OK, ___ uh, do you have time to grab a cup of coffee?
B OK. ___ That sounds good.

. . . .

A The coffee's good here.
B Yeah, I really like it. All right. ___ So, what did you want to talk about?
A Well, I wanted to ask a favor. I was wondering if you could help me with a survey.
B All right. ___ No problem.
A Great. Thanks. OK. ___ So, let me ask you a few questions about how you spend your time when you're with friends.
B All right. ___ Go ahead.

3 *Listening and speaking* *A small favor*

A Listen to four students ask their professor for a favor. Check (✔) what each student asks for.

	1. Peter	2. Sandra	3. Joel	4. Julia
a letter of recommendation	☐	☐	☐	☐
more time to finish a paper	☐	☐	☐	☐
permission to miss class for an interview	☐	☐	☐	☐
a signature on an application	☐	☐	☐	☐

B Listen again. Does the professor agree to their requests? Check (✔) yes or no. If you were the professor, which students would you say yes to?

1. Peter		2. Sandra		3. Joel		4. Julia	
Yes ☐	No ☐	Yes ☐	No ☐	Yes ☐	No ☐	Yes ☐	No ☐

About you → **C** *Pair work* Think of a favor you'd like to ask your partner. Take turns asking politely.

1 Reading

A Where can you read movie and CD reviews? Do you ever read them? Tell the class.

B Read the two reviews. Do the reviews encourage you to see the movie? buy the CD?

Home entertainment

DVD pick: *Madagascar*

Even though *Madagascar* might look like a movie for kids, the whole family can enjoy this animated film. The animation is wonderful, and the voices of the main characters – Marty the zebra (Chris Rock) and his three friends: Alex the lion (Ben Stiller), Melman the giraffe (David Schwimmer), and Gloria the hippo (Jada Pinkett Smith) – are outstanding.

The story begins in New York City's Central Park Zoo. Although Marty the zebra leads a comfortable life there, he dreams of living in the wild. Marty's friends seem happy in the zoo, especially Alex the lion, who enjoys the attention of all the visitors. He doesn't want to leave, and neither do Melman the giraffe and Gloria the hippo.

When Marty tries – and fails – to escape, the four friends end up on a boat to an animal preserve in Kenya. On the same boat are a group of penguins who want to go to Antarctica. The penguins hijack the boat, and, in the confusion, the friends fall into the ocean and wash up on a beach in Madagascar. There the zoo animals must learn to survive in a vast forest among lemurs and other animals.

Madagascar kept me laughing out loud – especially the penguins, who were my favorite characters. The film is so entertaining that even if you're not a fan of animated movies, you might want to see this one.

CD pick: *In the Heart of the Moon*
Ali Farka Touré and Toumani Diabaté

Even if you don't know anything about African music, I think you will enjoy this wonderful CD featuring two of Mali's most famous musicians: Toumani Diabaté on the *kora* (a traditional West African stringed instrument, similar to a harp or lute) and Ali Farka Touré on guitar.

In the Heart of the Moon is a beautifully recorded instrumental CD with a well-chosen mix of traditional and modern Malian tunes (one is said to be over 700 years old).

Music fans who have been following Diabaté's career and are used to his intense style may be surprised to hear a gentler, more mellow side to his playing here. His occasional rapid solos blend easily into the relaxed and sensuous playing of Touré's guitar.

If you haven't heard this CD yet, you have a real treat coming.

C Find the words on the left in the reviews. Use the context to match each word with a definition on the right.

1. in the wild ____
2. preserve ____
3. hijack ____
4. solo ____
5. blend ____
6. treat ____

a. take control of
b. a part of a song where one musician plays the most important part
c. an enjoyable experience
d. a place where animals are protected
e. in nature, the natural world
f. combine or mix together

D Read the reviews again, and answer the questions. Underline words and phrases in the reviews to support your answers. Then discuss your answers with a partner.

1. According to the reviewer, what age groups would enjoy *Madagascar*?
2. What are two things the reviewer really likes about the movie?
3. Which characters did the reviewer like best? Why?
4. What instruments do the musicians play on the CD *In the Heart of the Moon*?
5. What kinds of tunes are on the CD?
6. Why does the reviewer recommend the CD?

2 *Listening and writing* *I'd really recommend it.*

A Listen to Tom read a review of a Cirque du Soleil show. Does his friend want to see the show? Would you like to see it? Tell a partner.

B Listen again and check (✓) whether the sentences are true or false. Correct the false sentences.

	True	False
1. Cirque du Soleil performers are all Canadian.	☐	☐
2. The group started in Quebec over 20 years ago.	☐	☐
3. They now perform all over the world.	☐	☐
4. The acrobats perform with animals.	☐	☐
5. Tom has already seen a Cirque du Soleil show.	☐	☐
6. Tom is going to call to find out about tickets.	☐	☐

C Think of a show, a movie, a book, or a CD you have enjoyed. Write a review about it.

○○○   Document 1   ⊖

The Lion King

Even though I don't usually like musicals, I really loved *The Lion King.* The music and dancing are wonderful, and the costumes are simply amazing. Although the story may seem like it's for children, adults can really enjoy it, too.

If you haven't had a chance to see this fabulous musical yet, then go and buy tickets now!

▶ **Help note**

Contrasting ideas

Although the story may seem like it's for children, adults can really enjoy it, too.

Even though I don't usually enjoy animated movies, I loved this one.

Even if you don't know anything about African music, you'll enjoy this CD.

D *Class activity* Read your classmates' reviews. Can you find . . .

- a book you've been wanting to read?
- a movie you haven't seen yet?
- a play you'd like to see?
- a CD you've already heard?

3 *Free talk* *Who's been doing what?*

See *Free talk 10* for more speaking practice.

Vocabulary notebook

Great movies

Learning tip Linking new words to your experiences

When you learn a new word or expression, link it to something you have recently seen or done.

Movie or film?

People say **movie** 15 times more frequently than **film**.

movie

film

1 Match the types of movies to the movie titles.

1. an animated film _____
2. a thriller _____
3. a musical _____
4. a romantic comedy _____
5. a science-fiction movie _____

a. *2096: Living on Mars*
b. *Loving You Forever*
c. *The Spy Who Got Away*
d. *Funny Bunny*
e. *Singing in the Street*

2 Make a list of different types of movies. Link each one to a specific movie you have seen. Then write a sentence saying what the movie is about.

	Type of movie	Name of movie	What's it about?
1			
2			
3			
4			

3 Word builder Find out what kinds of movies these are. Put them in a chart like the one above. Can you think of the name of a movie for each one and say what it's about?

detective movie	fantasy film	historical drama	teen movie
documentary	gangster movie	martial-arts movie	western

On your own

Find a review in English of a new movie in a magazine or newspaper or on a Web site. What do you find out about the movie? Write a paragraph about it.

It's an animated film about robots.

It takes place in the future. It's pretty funny.

Impressions

In Unit 11, you learn how to . . .

- use the modal verbs *must*, *may*, *might*, *can't*, and *could* to speculate.
- use adjectives ending in *-ing* and *-ed* like *boring* and *bored*.
- talk about your impressions, feelings, and reactions.
- show you understand another person's feelings or situation.
- use *you see* to explain a situation.
- use *I see* to show you understand.

Before you begin . . .

What impressions do you get from each of these pictures? Make some guesses.

- How do you think the people in each picture are related to each other?
- What do you think is happening?
- How do you think each person feels?

Emma Hey, look. That girl over there must be
graduating.

Lloyd From college? Are you kidding? She can't
be more than 12.

Emma Well, she's wearing a cap and gown.

Lloyd Huh. She must be a genius.

Emma Sure, but she must study a lot, too.

Lloyd Yeah, probably all the time. I mean, she
can't have too many close friends here.
She's so much younger than everyone.

Emma Well, the guy she's talking to might be
one of her friends.

Lloyd He could be. Or he may be one of her
professors.

Emma True. . . . Oh, look. Those must be her
parents – the people with the cameras.

Lloyd Yeah. They must be feeling pretty proud.

1 Getting started

A 💿 Listen. Emma and Lloyd are speculating about the young girl at the graduation
ceremony. What guesses do they make?

Figure it out → **B** Can you complete these guesses with appropriate verbs?

1. The girl must _____ very smart.
2. There can't _____ many other college students who are that young.
3. The girl's parents must _____ lots of pictures today.
4. The students who are graduating might _____ sad to leave their friends.

2 Speaking naturally *Linking and deletion with* must

Before a vowel sound and /h, l, r, w, y/	**Before most consonant sounds**
She must enjoy school.	She mus(t) be a genius.
She must have some friends who are her age.	She mus(t) study all the time.
She must live with her parents.	She mus(t) feel lonely sometimes.

A 💿 Listen and repeat the sentences above. Practice linking the words as shown.

B Which of the speculations about the girl do you agree with? Can you add any more?
Tell the class.

3 Grammar *Modal verbs for speculating* 💿

She **must be** a genius.	=	*I bet she's a genius.*
She **must work** pretty hard.	=	*I bet she **works** pretty hard.*
She **must not go out** much.	=	*I bet she **doesn't go out** much.*
She **must be graduating** today.	=	*I bet she's **graduating** today.*
She **can't be** more than 12.	=	*It's not possible she's more than 12.*
He **could be** one of her friends.	=	*It's possible he's one of her friends.*
He **may be** her professor.	=	*Maybe he's her professor.*
They **might be feeling** sad.	=	*Maybe they're feeling sad.*

> **In conversation . . .**

Most uses of **must** and **might** – over 90% – are in affirmative statements. In negative statements, people usually say **must not** and **might not** with no contractions.

A What guesses can you make about the picture? Answer the questions with the modal verbs given: *must, may, might, can't,* or *could.*

1. What kind of ceremony is this?   It must . . .
2. What are the packets on the table?   They may / might / could . . .
3. Who is the man sitting in front of the table?   He may / might / could . . .
4. Why is the man shaking the woman's hand?   She must . . .
5. Is she graduating from elementary school?   She can't . . .
6. Who are the people sitting in the audience?   They must . . .

Useful language

graduation ceremony
college president
cap and gown
diploma

"It must be a graduation ceremony. People are wearing caps and gowns."

B *Pair work* Compare answers with a partner. What else can you say about the picture?

Ups and downs

Yoshi looks **bored**. **Tom** must be telling one of his **boring** stories. His stories are never **interesting**. **Sophia** seems **fascinated**, though. She must be **interested** in Tom.

Oh, no. **John** just spilled juice all over **Amy**. I bet he's **embarrassed**. She looks a bit **annoyed**. She can't be too **pleased** about her dress.

David just did something **embarrassing**. He locked his keys inside the car, and now he can't get in. That's so **frustrating**. He wanted to leave an hour ago. I bet he's **disappointed**.

What was that scream? Oh, there's a spider in **Jennifer**'s glass. She looks **shocked**. I think she's **scared** of spiders. **Ahmad** seems **surprised** by her reaction.

Andrea seems **excited** to see **Miguel**. She used to go out with him. Her new boyfriend, **Albert**, must be **jealous** and a little **anxious**. He may be **worried** that she'll go back to Miguel.

1 Building vocabulary and grammar

A 💿 Listen. Fred is describing the party to a friend. Can you identify each guest?

Word sort → **B** Complete the responses with adjectives from Fred's description of the party. More than one answer may be possible.

1. "Someone keeps calling me and then hanging up." "You must be _____ ."
2. "Tina and Ed just failed their driving tests for the third time!" "They must feel _____ ."
3. "My friend applied to graduate school, and he just got accepted." "He must feel _____ ."
4. "I'm the only one in my class who got an A on the test." "The other students must be _____ ."
5. "Jack just spilled coffee all over the teacher." "He must feel _____ ."
6. "My boyfriend hasn't called me for a week." "You must be _____ ."

Figure it out → **C** Can you complete the sentences with the adjectives given? Compare with a partner.

1. Yoshi isn't _____ in Tom's story. It's not an _____ story. (interesting, interested)
2. Sophia isn't _____ . She doesn't think Tom's story is _____ . (boring, bored)

2 Grammar *Adjectives ending in -ed and -ing*

Adjectives ending in -ed can describe how you feel about someone or something.	Adjectives ending in -ing can describe someone or something.
I'm **bored** with my job. I'm **interested** in astronomy. I get **annoyed** with my sister. I'm **excited** about my vacation. I'm **scared** of spiders.	My job is very **boring**. I think astronomy is **interesting**. She does a lot of **annoying** things. My vacation is going to be **exciting**. **But:** I think spiders are **scary**.

▶ **In conversation . . .**

Interesting, *interested*, *amazing*, *scary*, *surprised*, *worried*, *scared*, *excited*, *exciting*, and *boring* are all in the top 2,000 words.

A Choose the correct word to complete the sentences.

1. I'm really **excited / exciting** about my vacation. I'm going to Africa.
2. I'm **annoyed / annoying** with a friend of mine. He never returns my phone calls.
3. I saw a really **bored / boring** movie last night. I slept through most of it.
4. I wasn't able to get tickets to the concert. I was so **disappointed / disappointing**.
5. I get **frustrated / frustrating** when I try to read maps. I find them **confused / confusing**.
6. I get really **embarrassed / embarrassing** when I forget someone's name.
7. I heard something **amazed / amazing**. A woman just crossed the Pacific Ocean in a canoe.
8. My mother forgot my birthday. I was **surprised / surprising**. Well, actually, I was **shocked / shocking**.

About you

B *Pair work* Make the sentences above true for you. Have conversations.

A I'm really excited about my vacation. I'm going to India.
B That sounds really interesting. What are you going to do there?

3 Talk about it *Feelings*

Group work Discuss the questions. Write down any unusual and interesting responses, and then tell the class.

▶ Do you know anyone who is annoying? When is the last time you got annoyed with someone?
▶ Do you ever get bored? What kinds of things do you find boring?
▶ Are you scared of anything? Are there any movies that you find scary?
▶ Do you ever feel worried or anxious? What about?
▶ Have you ever felt really disappointed? What happened?
▶ Do you have any plans that you're excited about, like a party or a trip?
▶ What is the most exciting thing you've ever done?

4 Vocabulary notebook *How would you feel?*

See page 116 for a useful way to log and learn vocabulary.

That must be fun.

1 Conversation strategy *Showing you understand*

A Can you complete the responses to show you understand A's feelings or situation?

A *I've been studying Chinese for years, but I still can't read it well.*

B *You must be* _____ . **or** *That must be* _____ .

Now listen. Why hasn't Hal made much progress with his saxophone?

Debra	Hey, what's this saxophone doing here?
Hal	I have a lesson after work.
Debra	So, how long have you been playing?
Hal	Oh, a couple of years.
Debra	You must be getting pretty good by now.
Hal	I wish! I haven't made much progress lately.
Debra	Huh. How come?
Hal	Well, you see, I used to practice every morning. But then I started this job, and somehow I can't get myself to practice at night.
Debra	Well, you must be tired after work.
Hal	Yeah. But you know, I just joined a band.
Debra	That must be fun.
Hal	Yeah, it really is, and it keeps me motivated to practice. In fact, that's why I joined.
Debra	I see. Well, let me know if your band performs anywhere. I want to hear you play!

Notice how Debra uses *must* to show she understands Hal's situation or feelings. Find examples in the conversation.

"That must be fun."

B Think of a response to each sentence using *That must be* or *You must be* plus an adjective from the box. Then practice with a partner.

1. I've been taking dance lessons.   *"That must be fun."*
2. The elevator's not working, so I have to walk up to the tenth floor.
3. I just won a scholarship to go to college.
4. I often get up and study at 5:00 in the morning.
5. I'm going skydiving next week.
6. We're reading a book on ethics in my philosophy class.
7. I'm going out on a blind date tonight.

annoying	hard
bored	interesting
boring	motivated
excited	nervous
exciting	pleased
fascinating	proud
fun	scary
happy	tired

About you → **C** *Pair work* Write five sentences about yourself like the ones above. Take turns saying your sentences and reacting to them.

SELF-STUDY
AUDIO CD
CD-ROM

2 Strategy plus *You see* and *I see*

You can use **You see** to explain something that the other person might not know.

You can use **I see** to show you understand something that you didn't know earlier.

▶ **In conversation . . .**

I see and *you see* are in the top 900 words and expressions.

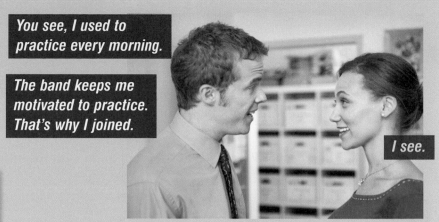

You see, I used to practice every morning.

The band keeps me motivated to practice. That's why I joined.

I see.

About you

Pair work Student A: Ask the questions. React to Student B's answers with *I see*, and continue the conversation. Student B: Answer the questions with true information. Explain your answers. Then change roles.

1. *A* Do you want to live abroad someday?
   B Yes, I really do. You see, . . . **or** Not really. You see, . . .

2. *A* Would you like to work less and have more time for fun?
   B I really would. You see, . . . **or** Not at all. You see, . . .

3. *A* Would you like to spend more time reading?
   B I think I would. You see, . . . **or** I don't think so. You see, . . .

A **Do you want to live abroad someday?**
B **Not really. You see, I'm a lawyer and I can't practice in another country.**
A **I see. So would you like to take a vacation in a foreign country?**

3 Listening *People and situations*

A 💿 Listen to the four conversations. Match each person with the situation he or she explains.

1. Mark _____   a. has always dreamed of studying art.
2. Angela _____   b. hasn't been studying a lot this year.
3. Linda _____   c. doesn't have enough time to practice.
4. David _____   d. wants to be able to talk to people while on vacation.

B 💿 Listen again. Show you understand. Write a response to each person using *must*.

1. _____   3. _____
2. _____   4. _____

4 Free talk *What on earth are they doing?*

See *Free talk 11* for more speaking practice.

1 Reading

A What are some things that people can volunteer to do in their communities? Do you know anyone who does volunteer work? What do they do?

B Read the article. What does Marcus try to do with his program, Just Say KNOW?

A TEEN HERO

He Coaches Kids – On and Off the Field

by John Garrity, *Sports Illustrated*

Standing in front of an eighth-grade class at Gove Middle School in Denver, 19-year-old Marcus Houston worked the audience like a seasoned[1] motivational speaker. "I can tell just by looking which of you are not going to be successful in life," he said, and then walked around the classroom studying faces. Kids who were slouched at their desks discreetly[2] straightened up.

"Aw, I'm just kidding," Marcus said with a grin. "But didn't you feel your heart stop? That's because you want to be successful."

Marcus uses his credibility as a star athlete (he was an all-state football player in high school) to motivate younger kids academically.

His concern began when he was a junior[3] at Denver's Thomas Jefferson High. Twelve freshman[4] footballers were flunking[5] classes and lost their eligibility. Disturbed by their failure and looking for an avenue of action, Houston created a program called Just Say KNOW. He went to middle schools, where he showed a football highlights video to capture the kids' imaginations, and then talked to them about the importance of being responsible and doing well in school.

"I think eighth grade is critical,"[6] Marcus says. "It's when kids develop their own vision[7] and decide what crowd they'll hang out with." He knew upperclassmen[8] could have a big impact on younger students. He is seeking corporate donations in hopes of taking Just Say KNOW national.

---

[1] *seasoned* experienced
[2] *discreetly* without attracting attention
[3] *junior* 11th-grade student
[4] *freshman* 9th-grade student
[5] *flunking* failing
[6] *critical* very important
[7] *vision* ideas about life
[8] *upperclassmen* 11th- or 12th-grade students

C Find the underlined expressions in the article. Match them with the definitions.

1. Marcus worked the audience. _____
2. Some kids were slouched at their desks. _____
3. Marcus uses his credibility as a star athlete. _____
4. Players who failed classes lost their eligibility. _____
5. Marcus was looking for an avenue of action. _____
6. Marcus hopes to take his program national. _____

a. not sitting up straight
b. were not allowed to play anymore
c. a way to make a difference
d. got the group's attention
e. create a national organization
f. the respect people have for him

2 *Listening and speaking* People making a difference

A Listen to the conversations. Match the people and the organizations they work with. Write *a*, *b*, or *c* next to their names.

① Janine Licare

② Arn Chorn-Pond

③ Ardena Gojani

a. The Cambodian Master Performers Program _____

b. The International Book Project _____

c. Kids Saving the Rainforest _____

B Listen again. Write what each organization does. Then compare answers with a partner. Which person are you most impressed with? Why?

C *Group work* Think of a volunteer program for your community. Who does it help? What does it do? Present your program to the class. Which programs should get "funding" – money from corporations or the government?

3 *Writing* A letter to the editor

A Here are two possible reactions to the article on page 114. Which do you agree with? Why? Tell a partner.

Dear Editor,
    It was exciting to read about a teen hero like Marcus Houston. It seems to me that many young people today are concerned mainly with their own interests and careers. I believe all teenagers should volunteer for programs like this....

Dear Editor,
    I was interested to read about Just Say KNOW. My impression is that many young people are really concerned about helping other people. In my opinion, the world can't be such a bad place with kids like Marcus making a difference....

B Write a letter to the editor about Marcus and his program or about the work of another person you admire. Use the letters above as models.

Dear Editor,
    I was very interested to read about ...

> **Help note**
>
> **Impressions, reactions, and opinions**
>
> *My impression is that . . .*
> *It seems to me that . . .*
> *I think / believe / feel that . . .*
> *In my opinion / view, . . .*

C *Group work* Read your classmates' letters. Are people's reactions similar? Did you learn about any interesting people and projects?

How would you feel?

Learning tip *Linking situations and feelings*

When you learn words for feelings, link them to different situations where you might experience each one.

1 How would you feel in each situation? Complete the sentences. Use the adjectives in the box or other words you know.

annoyed   bored   disappointed   scared

1. *You're in class. You've finished your work, and there's nothing else to do.*

   I'd probably feel _____ .

2. *You are waiting for a friend at a restaurant, and the friend calls to say he or she can't meet you.*

   I think I'd be _____ .

3. *A friend borrowed some of your CDs and returned them scratched.*

   I'd feel _____ .

4. *You're on a dark and quiet street, and someone is following you.*

   I'd feel _____ .

2 Think of situations for these different emotions. Complete the sentences.

1. I feel very motivated to practice my English when _____ .

2. I think it's annoying when _____ .

3. I was really shocked once when _____ .

4. Sometimes I get frustrated when _____ .

5. I think it's embarrassing when _____ .

6. Sometimes I get confused when _____ .

3 *Word builder* Can you make sentences with each pair of adjectives?

1. astonished / astonishing _____

2. upset / upsetting _____

3. terrified / terrifying _____

4. thrilled / thrilling _____

On your own

This week, take some time to observe the people around you. Notice what they are doing, and try to guess how they feel. Write 5–10 sentences in your notebook.

In the news

In Unit 12, you learn how to . . .

- use the simple past passive in news stories.
- talk about local and international news events.
- talk about extreme weather and natural disasters.
- introduce news in conversation with expressions like *Guess what?*
- use expressions like *The thing is . . .* to introduce issues.

Before you begin . . .

- How do you find out about what's going on in the world?
- Which aspects of the news are you most interested in?
- What major events are in the news right now?

Ruth Anything interesting in the paper?

Jack Oh, not much. Let's see. Uh, $10,000 was found in a bag on a city bus.

Ruth $10,000? I should ride the bus more often!

Jack Yeah, and listen to this. Two large bears were seen last night in someone's yard.

Ruth Huh. That's kind of scary.

Jack Oh, and a jewelry store was broken into, and some diamonds were stolen. Um, what else? The city airport was closed yesterday because of strong winds.

Ruth Really? Well, it was pretty windy.

Jack Yeah. All the flights were delayed. Oh, and a bus was hit by a falling tree. Fortunately, the passengers weren't hurt.

Ruth Is that all? Nothing exciting, I guess.

Getting started

A Listen. Jack tells Ruth some news from the local newspaper. Complete the headlines.

❶ **Student finds** _____ **on bus**

❷ **Teen sees bears in** _____

❸ **THIEF BREAKS INTO** _____ **, TAKES** _____

❹ **AIRPORT CLOSES BECAUSE OF** _____

❺ **Falling tree hits** _____

Figure it out

B Which sentences about the news stories are true? Correct the false ones.

	True	False
1. A bag of money was stolen on a bus.	☐	☐
2. Two bears were seen in a house.	☐	☐
3. The airport was closed.	☐	☐
4. Flights were canceled.	☐	☐

2 Grammar *The simple past passive*

Use the active form of a verb to focus on the "doer" or cause of the action.	Use the passive form to focus on the "receiver" of the action, or when the "doer" or cause is not known or not important.
A student **found** a bag on a bus.	A bag **was found** on a bus.
The authorities **closed** the airport.	The airport **was closed**.
A teenager **saw** two bears in a yard.	Two bears **were seen** in a yard.
The accident **didn't injure** the passengers.	The passengers **weren't injured**.

▶ *In conversation . . .*

The passive is approximately 5 times more common in written news than in conversation, but people often use the passive to talk about news events.

A Rewrite the sentences. Use the simple past passive.

1. Someone saw a snake on the subway.

   <u>A snake was seen on the subway.</u>

2. Someone sold a famous painting for $6,000,000.

   _____

3. Someone left hundreds of pineapples on the sidewalk yesterday.

   _____

4. Someone broke into a store and stole some soccer balls.

   _____

5. Someone found a diamond ring in a doughnut.

   _____

6. They canceled school throughout the city yesterday.

   _____

B *Pair work* Take turns telling the news items above. Use your own ideas, and ask questions. Who can think of the strangest story?

A ***A snake was seen on the subway yesterday.***
B ***No kidding! What happened exactly?***
A ***Well, the subway was closed for two hours. The snake was caught and . . .***

3 Speaking naturally *Breaking sentences into parts*

Ten thousand dollars / was found in a bag / on a city bus.
Two large bears / were seen last night / in someone's yard.
A jewelry store / was broken into, / and some diamonds were stolen.
The city airport / was closed yesterday / because of strong winds.

A Listen and repeat the sentences above. Notice how sentences with a lot of new information are broken into shorter parts. One syllable in each part receives the strongest stress.

B Practice the conversation on page 118. Take turns playing Jack's role. Break Jack's sentences into shorter parts with a single stress as shown above.

Lesson B Natural disasters

1 Building vocabulary and grammar

A Listen. Which picture goes with each news item? Number the pictures.

1 The island of Puerto Rico was **hit** by **Hurricane** Calvin late this morning. Electric power was temporarily **disrupted** throughout the island, and many homes were **damaged** by **heavy rains** and **strong winds**.

2 Quebec was hit by **severe thunderstorms** yesterday. Flights at several airports were delayed by heavy rains, **thunder**, and **lightning**. Last night, three families were **rescued** by emergency workers after their homes were damaged by **flash floods** resulting from the rains.

3 Firefighters in Australia say over 10,000 acres of forest were completely **destroyed** by **catastrophic wildfires** this year. Investigators suspect some fires were caused by careless campers. They believe other fires started when trees were **struck** by lightning.

4 A shopping mall in Kansas was badly damaged by a **tornado** last night. A nearby town was later hit by a **freak hailstorm**. Cars were struck by **hailstones** the size of golf balls. Amazingly, no one was seriously **injured** by the tornado or the storm.

5 A small town in Italy was struck by a **minor earthquake** this morning. The quake measured 4.9 on the Richter scale. **Aftershocks** were felt in several towns. Some homes were partially destroyed, but no serious injuries were reported.

Word sort

B Write words and expressions from the news stories that go with each category below. Compare lists with a partner.

Earth	Wind	Fire	Water
earthquake (quake) struck by an earthquake	tornado damaged by a tornado		

Figure it out

C Can you put these statements in the correct order? Compare with a partner.

1. firefighters / rescued / two families / by / were
2. was / hailstones / struck / a car / by
3. injured / was / seriously / no one
4. completely / a mall / destroyed / was / by / a fire

120

2 Grammar *The simple past passive with by + agent*

When the agent – the "doer" of the action – is important, you can use **by** to introduce it.	Adverbs with the passive
Three families were rescued **by** emergency workers. The fires were caused **by** careless campers. A shopping mall was damaged **by** a tornado.	A mall was **badly** damaged. No one was **seriously** injured. The forest was **completely** destroyed. Power was **temporarily** disrupted. Homes were **partially** destroyed.

A Write the first sentence of a news story for each headline. Use the passive with *by* + agent and an adverb. Add details to explain where and when each story happened.

❶ Fire destroys old warehouse

An old warehouse was partially destroyed by a fire in Miami last night.

❷ Earthquake disrupts water service and electric power

_____

_____

❸ HURRICANE DAMAGES HIGH SCHOOL

_____

_____

❹ LIGHTNING INJURES TWO GOLFERS

_____

_____

❺ Tornado destroys police station

_____

_____

B *Group work* Add a few sentences to one of the news stories above to write a short TV news report. Read your report to the class. Which story is the most interesting?

3 Listening and speaking *News update*

A Listen to two news stories. Answer the questions.

1. What kinds of weather does the reporter talk about? _____
2. What problems did the weather cause? _____
3. Who were the people rescued by? _____
4. Why was the wedding canceled? _____
5. What happened to the groom? _____
6. What update on the story does the reporter give? _____

B *Pair work* Create your own news story. Role-play a TV news anchor and a reporter. Practice your story, and then act it out for the class.

4 Vocabulary notebook *Forces of nature*

See page 126 for a useful way to log and learn vocabulary.

1 Conversation strategy   *Telling news*

A Put the conversation in the correct order. Number the sentences from 1 to 5.

____ *Yeah. Well, she was robbed last night.*
____ *Well, you know that tall woman, Annie?*
____ *Did you hear the news?*
____ *Yeah. The one who works in the café?*
____ *No. What happened?*

🎧 **Now listen.** What happened in Joey and Celia's neighborhood last night?

Joey	Did you hear about all the trouble here last night?
Celia	No, but I heard some police sirens.
Joey	Well, you know that older guy on the first floor of my building?
Celia	Yeah. . . .
Joey	Guess what? His car was stolen.
Celia	That's terrible.
Joey	And you know what? He heard his car alarm and called the police, but they came way too late.
Celia	I'm not surprised. The thing is, they just don't have enough police on duty at night.
Joey	Exactly.
Celia	Oh, and did I tell you? My car was broken into last Thursday night.
Joey	No. Really? Was anything stolen?
Celia	No. The only thing was, they damaged the ignition trying to start the car, . . . but the funny thing was, they couldn't start it because the battery was dead!

Notice how Joey and Celia introduce news with expressions like these. Find examples in the conversation.

Did you hear (about) . . . ?	*Guess what?*
Have you heard (about) . . . ?	*You know what?*
Did I tell you?	*You know . . . ?*

B Match the questions with the news they introduce. Compare answers with a partner.

1. I just bought a new TV. And you know what? _____
2. Did I tell you about my accident? _____
3. Did you hear about the tornado? _____
4. I won a talent contest. And guess what? _____
5. Have you heard the good news about John? _____
6. You know the woman who lives next door? _____

a. I fell off the roof of the house.
b. He's getting married in the spring.
c. She's a friend of my cousin's.
d. It's broken already.
e. I'm going to be on television.
f. It destroyed the mall.

About you → **C** *Pair work* Take turns telling your own news, using the expressions above.

SELF-STUDY
AUDIO CD
CD-ROM

2 Strategy plus *The . . . thing is / was*

Use ***The . . . thing is / was*** to introduce ideas.

The thing is / was . . . **(to identify a key issue)**
The other thing is . . . **(to add another issue)**
The only thing is . . . **(to raise a problem)**

Add adjectives to introduce other ideas.

The best thing is / was . . .
The funny thing is . . .
The scary thing is . . .

> The thing is, they just don't have enough police on duty at night.

> **In conversation . . .**

Here are the most common expressions with ***The . . . thing is / was***:

The thing is . . .
The other thing is . . .
The only thing is . . .
The (adjective) thing is . . .

A Complete the sentences with an appropriate word or expression from the box. Compare with a partner.

best thing	only thing	scary thing
funny thing	other thing	thing

1. I loved everything about my vacation, but the _____ was, the weather was perfect.
2. I'm a little bored with my job. The _____ is, I'm not learning anything new, and the _____ is, I don't have much in common with my co-workers.
3. My car was stolen once. The _____ was, they brought it back the next day.
4. My new boyfriend is great in almost every way. The _____ is, he gossips too much.
5. I was in a small earthquake once. The _____ was, I didn't know what to do.

About you → **B** *Pair work* Change the sentences above to make them true for you.

"I love everything about my new apartment, but the best thing is, I have a great view."

3 Listening *What do they say next?*

A Read the last lines of four conversations. Can you guess what each conversation is about?

☐ *"The thing is, people need to feel safe when they go out at night."*

☐ *"The scary thing was, we didn't have electricity for three days."*

☐ *"And you know what? Everything was gone – her money, credit cards, keys, everything."*

☐ *"So the funny thing is, her prediction about her car turned out to be true."*

B 💿 Listen to the beginning of each conversation. Choose an ending above. Number the sentences.

C 💿 Now listen to the complete conversations, and check your answers.

1 Reading

A Brainstorm! How many different ways do people get the news? Add ideas to the word web. In your opinion, what's the best way?

watch cable TV ———— **ways people get the news** ———— read a newspaper

B Read the article. What is *OhmyNews*? How is it different?

A new brand of journalism is taking root in South Korea

By Dan Gillmor – *San Jose Mercury News*

SEOUL – Lee Bong-Ryul has a day job as an engineer at a semiconductor company. In his spare time, he's helping to shape tomorrow's journalism.

Lee is an active "citizen-reporter" for *OhmyNews*, an online news service. *OhmyNews* is transforming the 20th-century's journalism-as-lecture model, where organizations tell the audience what the news is, and the audience either buys it or doesn't, into something vastly more bottom-up, interactive, and democratic.

In South Korea, the Internet is a part of everyday life. More than two-thirds of households are connected to the Internet, most with high-speed links.

Even taxi drivers who don't have time for newspapers have heard of *OhmyNews*. The site draws millions of visitors daily. Advertisers are supporting both the Korean-language Web site (www.ohmynews.com) and a weekly print edition,[1] and the operation has been profitable in recent months, according to its chief executive and founder, Oh Yeon-Ho.

Oh is a 38-year-old former writer for progressive magazines. With a staff[2] of about 50 and legions[3] of "citizen-reporter" contributors – more than 26,000 have signed up, and more than 15,000 have published stories under their bylines[4] – Oh and his colleagues are creating something entirely new.

"The main concept is that every citizen can be a reporter," he says.

The site posts about 70 percent of the roughly 200 items submitted each day, after staff editors look

Oh Yeon-Ho

at the stories. What's so different here is that anyone can sign up, and it's not difficult to get published. The Web means space for news is essentially unlimited, and *OhmyNews* welcomes contributions from just about anyone.

The citizen-reporters do cover politics, economy, culture, arts, and science – the usual subjects you'll find in newspapers – but they tend to focus more on personally oriented issues like education, job conditions, and the environment.

While about 85 percent of the online edition is written by the citizen-reporters, about 90 percent of the weekly print edition is written by the staff.

OhmyNews' ambitions aren't limited to mere words. It runs video Webcasting services and plans to expand its multimedia presence. Someday, citizen-reporters could be contributing video reports.

OhmyNews is an experiment in tomorrow. So far, it's looking like a brilliant one.

[1] *print edition*   newspaper
[2] *staff*   group of employees
[3] *legions*   large numbers
[4] *byline*   the writer's name at the beginning of a news story

C Read the article again. Are these sentences true or false?
Correct the false statements.

	True	False
1. The majority of South Koreans have access to the Internet.	☐	☐
2. *OhmyNews* plays an important role in reporting the news in South Korea.	☐	☐
3. Only professional journalists write the online news reports.	☐	☐
4. *OhmyNews* publishes all the articles that the reporters post.	☐	☐
5. In addition to the online Web site, there is a printed paper version of *OhmyNews*.	☐	☐
6. Unlike other news services, *OhmyNews* only covers personal issues.	☐	☐

2 Speaking and writing *Are you up on the news?*

A *Class activity* Survey your classmates and find out their news habits. Keep a record
of their answers, and then tally (卌ǀ) the results.

NEWS SURVEY

1. How often do you keep up with the news?

every day [ ]   once or twice a week [ ]   less than once a week [ ]

2. Where do you usually get the news?

TV [ ]   newspapers [ ]   Internet [ ]

radio [ ]   magazines [ ]   other _____ [ ]

3. What news are you most interested in?

local [ ]   national [ ]   international [ ]

4. What three topics are you most interested in?

current events [ ]   sports [ ]   business [ ]   science and technology [ ]

celebrities [ ]   the arts [ ]   the weather [ ]   other _____ [ ]

B Use the information from your survey to write a report about the class's interest
in the news.

○○○　　　　Document 1

News Survey

Almost 80% of the students in this class
keep up with the news every day. About
20% of us keep up with the news only
once or twice a week. Approximately
two out of three students watch the
news on TV. . . .

▶ **Help note**

Writing about statistics

80% of the students are interested in the news.
80% of the class is interested in the news.
Approximately 20% of us get the news from TV.
The majority of students have access to the Internet.
About half of the class is interested in current events.
Four out of ten students read a newspaper.

C *Pair work* Read a partner's report. Do you agree on your findings? What information
from the survey is most surprising? Why?

3 Free talk *Here's the news!*

See **Free talk 12** for more speaking practice.

Forces of nature

Learning tip Collocations

When you learn a new word, use a dictionary to find out what other words are typically used with it. For example, you can say *flash floods*, but not usually *quick floods*. Or you can say *seriously injured*, but not usually *completely injured*.

> **Cold weather**
>
> In the U.S. and Canada, the 6 most frequent adjectives people say before the word ***weather*** are:
>
> 1. cold   4. good
> 2. nice   5. warm
> 3. bad   6. hot

1 Look at the adjectives on the left. Circle the word that is typically used with each one.

1. **freak**	rain	(hailstorm)	earthquake
2. **heavy**	wildfire	tornado	rain
3. **minor**	earthquake	rain	wind
4. **flash**	tornado	earthquake	flood
5. **catastrophic**	thunder	wildfire	hailstones

2 *Word builder* For each sentence below, cross out the one word that *cannot* be used to complete it.

1. A building was _____ by lightning.
   a. damaged   b. destroyed   c. injured   d. struck   e. hit

2. _____ was disrupted by an ice storm yesterday.
   a. Electrical power   b. A shopping mall   c. Traffic   d. Telephone service   e. Train service

3. Two people were _____ injured.
   a. seriously   b. critically   c. severely   d. partially   e. slightly

4. The village was struck by _____ .
   a. an earthquake   b. lightning   c. a hurricane   d. hailstones   e. rain

3 *Word builder* Look at the expressions below. Can you figure out their meanings?

freak accident   **heavy traffic**   **major earthquake**   **minor injuries**

On your own

Think of 3 places in different parts of the world. Go online and find out what the weather is like today.

Honolulu
92°F
33°C
Mostly sunny

1 What can you guess about Suki?

A Look at the pictures of Suki's apartment. What has she been doing? What has she finished? Complete each sentence with the present perfect or present perfect continuous.

There are two pots on the stove, so I think she __'s been cooking__ (cook). She _____ already _____ (bake) some cookies. She _____ (write) a letter, but she _____ (not finish) it yet. There's a whole pizza, so I bet she _____ (not eat) lunch. There are two CDs on the table, so she _____ probably _____ (listen) to music. Her paints and brushes are out, so it looks like she _____ (paint). She already _____ (paint) a vase of flowers.

B Pair work Make more guesses about Suki and the pictures. Use *must, may, might, can't,* or *could*.

"She must like pizza."   *"She might be an art teacher."*

2 That must be interesting!

Complete A's statements with *since, for,* or *in,* and add an adjective to B's responses. Practice with a partner. Then practice again, making the sentences true for you.

1. *A* I've been taking dance lessons _____ I was a kid.   *B* You must be _____ .
2. *A* I haven't heard from my boyfriend _____ ages.   *B* You must be _____ .
3. *A* I've been going out with someone _____ several months now. *B* That must be _____ .
4. *A* I've been working hard _____ May. I haven't had a vacation. *B* That must be _____ .

"I've been taking piano lessons since I was five."   *"You must be really good."*

3 Have you seen any good movies lately?

Complete the chart with three movies you've seen. Discuss with a partner.

Name of movie	Type of movie	What it was like
My Best Friend's Wedding	a romantic comedy	It was very funny.
1.		
2.		
3.		

A **Have you seen any good movies lately?**
B **Yeah. I saw My Best Friend's Wedding. It's a romantic comedy. It was very funny.**
A **What's it about?**

127

4 Can you complete this conversation?

Complete the conversation with the words and expressions in the box.
Use capital letters where necessary.

yet	✓ guess what	that must be	the thing is	I was wondering
already	you know what	all right	the only thing is	I see

Ana <u>Guess what</u> ? We have a new boss – Abigail Freeman.
       And _____ ? Things are going to change around here!

Nat Really? So, have you met her _____ ?

Ana No, but I've _____ heard lots of stories about her.
       _____ , she's a "clean freak." She hates clutter. So everyone
       is busy cleaning and putting things away.

Nat _____ . So I guess we're going to have to clean up this mailroom.

Ana Actually, _____ if we could start now because she might come by later.

Nat Yeah. We need to make a good first impression. _____ , every time
       I clean up, I lose something!

Ana Really? _____ frustrating! So let's be careful when we throw things away!

Nat Good idea. _____ , let's get started!

5 I was wondering . . .

Pair work Think of two more favors to add to the list below. Then think of a way
to ask politely for each favor. Role-play conversations.

1. Ask a teacher for more time to finish an assignment.   3. _____
2. Ask a friend to give you a ride to the airport.   4. _____

A Excuse me. I was wondering if I could have more time to finish my assignment.
B Well, can you tell me why you need more time?

6 Here's the news.

A Complete the news report. Use the simple past passive.

Four cars _____ (involve) in an accident on the freeway
this morning. The accident _____ (cause) by a truck
that spilled hundreds of tomatoes onto the road. Fortunately, the
drivers _____ seriously _____ (not injure). Two people
_____ (take) to the hospital with minor injuries. The
truck driver _____ (interview) by police. The freeway
_____ (open) again two hours later.

B Pair work Brainstorm words and expressions describing extreme
weather and natural disasters. Then write five sentences to create a
news report. Read your report to the class.

severe thunderstorm	heavy rains

Self-check
How sure are you about these areas?
Circle the percentages.

grammar
20% 40% 60% 80% 100%
vocabulary
20% 40% 60% 80% 100%
conversation strategies
20% 40% 60% 80% 100%

. . . .

Study plan
What do you want to review?
Circle the lessons.

grammar
10A 10B 11A 11B 12A 12B
vocabulary
10A 10B 11A 11B 12A 12B
conversation strategies
10C 11C 12C

Free talk 1   People are interesting!

Class activity What interesting things can you find out about your classmates? Ask questions and take notes. Tell the class something new you learned about two classmates.

Find someone who . . .	Name	Notes
reads very fast.	Kenji	reads the whole newspaper in 20 minutes
eats extremely slowly.		
is pretty competitive.		
is incredibly organized.		
can do math in his / her head quickly.		
remembers people's names easily.		
thinks it's important to dress properly.		
automatically turns on the TV at night.		
immediately gets out of bed in the morning.		
plays several sports very well.		

A **Do you read very fast, Kenji?**
B **Yeah, pretty fast. I read the whole newspaper in about 20 minutes.**

Free talk 2   Can you believe it? I've never done that!

Group game Are there things you've *never* done that you think people in your group *have* done? Complete the chart and then compare answers. Give yourself 1 point for each group member who *has* done the thing you haven't done. The person with the most points wins.

Think of . . .	I've never . . .	How many students have done this?
a food you've never eaten.	I've never eaten fish.	2
something you've never drunk.		
a TV show you've never seen.		
a sport you've never played.		
a city or country you've never been to.		
a kind of music you've never listened to.		
a place in your town you've never visited.		
something else you've never done.		
	Total points	

A **I've never eaten fish.**
B **You're kidding! I've eaten fish all my life.**
C **Me too. I eat fish every week.**
D **I haven't. I've always been a vegetarian.**
A **OK. That gives me 2 points.**

1 Group work Write your country's name at the top of the chart. Discuss the categories and agree on the most special wonder for each one. Give reasons for your choices. Complete the chart.

The five greatest wonders of		Reasons
☐ beautiful natural feature		
☐ ancient city or monument		
☐ modern human wonder		
☐ interesting museum		
☐ popular tourist attraction		

2 Group work Rank the five wonders from one to five (1 = the most special). Compare your group's wonders with the rest of the class.

1 Prepare a short history of your family. Use these ideas to help you.

> ***Think about . . .***
>
> *where your grandparents are from.*
> *interesting facts about your aunts and uncles.*
> *how your parents met.*
> *where your parents used to live when they were younger.*
> *how your family life has changed.*
> *any special memories you have.*

_____

_____

_____

_____

_____

_____

2 Group work Present your family history to the group. Listen to your classmates' histories. Take notes and ask them questions for more information.

"My father's parents are from Acapulco. They moved to Mexico City in 1964. My father grew up there. . . . My mother's parents . . ."

Do we have enough for the party?

Group work Imagine your group is having a party for 15 people. You've just gone shopping. Do you have everything you need? First, make a list of what you have. Then discuss these questions, and make a new shopping list.

- Do you have enough of everything?
- Do you have too much of anything?
- Do you need anything else?
- Is there anything you don't need?

What we have:	Shopping list – What we need to buy:
8 packages of popcorn	

A **We have eight packages of popcorn.**
B **I think we bought too much popcorn.**
C **Yeah. We only need two or three packages.**

1 *Group work* Imagine you are organizing an event together. Choose one of the possibilities below, or think of your own event. Make a "to do" list of all the things you need to do to get ready for it.

a class trip to a nearby city for the weekend

a garage sale to get rid of all your unwanted things

a picnic for a group of your friends

A I think we should organize a class trip.
B Actually, I'd rather plan a picnic. What do you think?
C I think I'd rather have a picnic, too.

TO DO:

Useful language

We might want to . . .
We should . . .
We ought to . . .
We'd better . . .

We're going to have to . . .
We've got to . . .
We have to . . .

I'd rather (not) . . .

Who's going to   bring . . . ?
make a reservation for . . . ?
research . . . on the Internet?

I'll bring . . .

2 *Class activity* Tell the class about your event. What are you going to do? Where are you going to go? Which event would you like to attend?

Free talk 7   What's important?

Group work What should you consider when you choose a life partner? Discuss these ideas and add your own. Agree on the five most important things, and tell the class.

You should choose someone . . .

- who has a good sense of humor.
- that your family likes.
- who comes from a similar background.
- that you can talk to about anything.
- who is very good-looking.

- who has similar interests.
- that you can trust.
- who is kind and generous.
- who has a good job.
- who has a lot of money.

The five most important things to consider
1.
2.
3.
4.
5.

A *Well, I think you should choose someone who has a good sense of humor.*
B *That's true. Relationships can be difficult. You need to be able to laugh sometimes.*
C *I agree. I went out with a guy who didn't have a sense of humor, and it was boring.*

Free talk 9A   Tech trivia

Pair work Student A: Ask your partner the questions below. How many right answers can he or she get? Then answer your partner's questions.

Questions	Answers	Right	Wrong
1. Can you tell me what **www** stands for?	World Wide Web.	☐	☐
2. Do you know which country has the fastest computer?	Japan.	☐	☐
3. Do you know what the world's most visited Web site is?	AOL.com.	☐	☐
4. Do you know what the most searched-for flower on Google is?	The rose.	☐	☐
5. Can you tell me what the past tense of **download** is?	Downloaded.	☐	☐
6. Can you tell me how to spell **database**?	D-A-T-A-B-A-S-E.	☐	☐
7. Can you tell me what **PLS** means in a text message?	Please.	☐	☐
8. Do you know who invented the World Wide Web?	Tim Berners-Lee.	☐	☐

Free talk 8 — What would you do?

Group work Discuss the questions. How are you alike? How are you different? Who has the most interesting answer for each question?

1. If you had an hour to spare right now, what would you do?
2. If you had one month of free time, what would you do?
3. If you had to choose one thing to carry with you through life, what would it be?
4. If you had to choose one electronic gadget to live without, what would it be?
5. If you could invite a famous person to a party, who would you invite?
6. If you could be like one person, who would you want to be like?
7. If you could choose any job, what kind of work would you do?
8. If you could have one special talent, what would it be?
9. If you had to give up one habit, what would it be?
10. If you had one wish, what would you wish for?

A *If I had an hour to spare right now, I'd take a nap. I'm kind of tired.*
B *Not me. I'd go for a run in the park. I need some exercise.*
C *Yeah? I'd go shopping at the mall. I need some new shoes.*

Free talk 9B — Tech trivia

Pair work Student B: Ask your partner the questions below. How many right answers can he or she get? Then answer your partner's questions.

Questions	Answers	Right	Wrong
1. Can you tell me what **DVD** stands for?	Digital Video Disc.	☐	☐
2. Do you know which country has the most Internet users?	The United States.	☐	☐
3. Do you know what city has the biggest Internet café?	New York City.	☐	☐
4. Do you know what the most searched-for animal on Google is?	The cat.	☐	☐
5. Can you tell me what the past tense of **input** is?	Input or inputted.	☐	☐
6. Can you tell me how to spell **cyberspace**?	C-Y-B-E-R-S-P-A-C-E.	☐	☐
7. Can you tell me what **THNQ** means in a text message?	Thank you.	☐	☐
8. Do you know who invented the telephone?	Antonio Meucci.	☐	☐

Who's been doing what?

Class activity Find classmates who answer yes to the questions. Write their names in the chart. Write notes about each person. Tell the class two interesting things you learned.

Find someone who's been . . .	Name	Notes
spending a lot of time shopping lately.	Ana	has been going to the mall every weekend
saving money to buy something special.		
working too hard lately.		
taking an evening class.		
going to the movies a lot.		
planning a special occasion or event.		
watching too much TV this month.		
planning a vacation.		
reading a really good book.		
working out a lot lately.		

A **Ana, have you been spending a lot of time shopping lately?**

B **Yeah, I have. I've been going to the mall every weekend.**

What on earth are they doing?

Pair work Can you guess what the people are doing in the pictures below? Write three sentences about each picture. Discuss your ideas with a partner. Do you agree?

"I think they must be practicing . . . because . . ."

1 *Pair work* Make up a short TV news report about each picture. Think of three facts for each story.

2 *Group work* Join another pair. Take turns telling your news stories. Are any of your stories the same?

Self-study listening

Unit 1

A *Track 1* Listen to the conversation on page 6. Alexis and Jacob are talking about Jacob's roommate.

B *Track 2* Listen to the rest of their conversation. Check (✓) true or false for each sentence.

	True	False
1. Kim is Alexis's old roommate.	☐	☒
2. Kim talks to Alexis a lot.	☒	☐
3. Kim is always saying mean things.	☐	☐
4. Kim's friends are always visiting their apartment.	☒	☐
5. Alexis is always giving Kim free tickets.	☐	☐
6. Alexis likes her new roommate.	☐	☐

Unit 2

A *Track 3* Listen to the conversation on page 16. Debra and Hal are talking about movies they like.

B *Track 4* Listen to the rest of their conversation. Circle the correct words.

1. Debra wants to see the Will Smith movie at **6:00** / **9:30**.
2. Hal wants to eat **before** / **after** the movie.
3. Debra **likes** / **doesn't like** sci-fi movies.
4. Hal now wants to see the **Will Smith** / **Bruce Willis** movie.
5. Hal **will** / **won't** finish his work before the movie.

Unit 3

A *Track 5* Listen to the conversation on page 26. Kim and Juan are hiking.

B *Track 6* Listen to the rest of their conversation. Choose the right answer. Circle *a* or *b*.

1. How tall are the sequoias?
   a. The height of a 26-story building.
   b. The height of a 62-story building.

2. How old are the oldest sequoias?
   a. About 300 years old.
   b. About 3,000 years old.

3. How old is the oldest tree?
   a. Almost 4,000 years old.
   b. Almost 5,000 years old.

4. Where is the oldest tree?
   a. Near Sequoia National Park.
   b. In Sequoia National Park.

5. Why does Juan know so much about trees?
   a. Studying trees is his hobby.
   b. He read about them in his guidebook.

Unit 4

A *Track 7* Listen to the conversation on page 38. Rob and Paula are talking about their kids.

B *Track 8* Listen to the rest of their conversation. Check (✓) true or false for each sentence.

	True	False
1. Paula's family used to spend weekends together.	☐	☐
2. Rob used to play baseball with his dad.	☐	☐
3. Paula is always driving her kids somewhere.	☐	☐
4. Rob wants everyone to come to a barbecue next weekend.	☐	☐
5. Paula is going to take her kids home now.	☐	☐

SSL1

Unit 5

A *Track 9* Listen to the conversation on page 48. Laura and Kayla are at Laura's apartment.

B *Track 10* Listen to the rest of their conversation. Circle the correct words.

1. Kayla is having **hot** / **iced** tea.
2. **Laura** / **Laura's mother** made the cookies.
3. The cookies don't have much **fat** / **sugar**.
4. The cookies are **lemon** / **ginger** and chocolate.
5. Kayla **likes** / **doesn't like** the cookies.
6. Kayla wants to have **some cake** / **another cookie**.

Unit 6

A *Track 11* Listen to the conversation on page 58. Ramon and Ling are talking on the phone.

B *Track 12* Listen to their conversation later that evening. Check (✓) true or false for each sentence.

	True	False
1. Ramon is at the gym.	☐	☐
2. Ling has another seminar on Saturday.	☐	☐
3. Ling and Ramon had plans to meet on Saturday.	☐	☐
4. Ramon wants Ling to go to the seminar.	☐	☐
5. Ling decides not to go to class on Saturday.	☐	☐
6. Ramon is going to call Ling back.	☐	☐

Unit 7

A *Track 13* Listen to the conversation on page 70. Maria and Chen are in the hallway of Maria's apartment building.

B *Track 14* Listen to the rest of their conversation. Check (✓) true or false for each sentence.

	True	False
1. Chen is talking about the guy who lives next to him.	☐	☐
2. The neighbor gave Chen a key to his apartment.	☐	☐
3. Maria thinks it's good that neighbors can help each other out.	☐	☐
4. Chen's neighbor needed his key at 2:00 a.m.	☐	☐
5. Chen complained to his neighbor.	☐	☐
6. Chen is going to help his neighbor again next week.	☐	☐

Unit 8

A *Track 15* Listen to the conversation on page 80. Nicole and Carlos are talking on campus.

B *Track 16* Listen to the rest of their conversation. Choose the right answer. Circle *a* or *b*.

1. Nicole is thinking about living _____ .
   a. in a student dormitory
   b. with her aunt and uncle

2. Nicole's aunt and uncle used to _____ .
   a. have a student living with them
   b. have a relative living with them

3. Nicole has applied _____ .
   a. only to Bracken Tech
   b. to several schools

4. Carlos would like to live _____ .
   a. with Nicole's relatives
   b. with Nicole's friends

5. Carlos has _____ .
   a. met Nicole's relatives before
   b. never met Nicole's relatives

6. Nicole's uncle and Carlos _____ .
   a. both like baseball
   b. both like engineering

Unit 9

A *Track 17* Listen to the conversation on page 90. Jacob and Greg are in their apartment.

B *Track 18* Listen to the rest of their conversation. Circle the correct words.

1. Greg is looking at a **chat room** / **Web site** for inventors.
2. One guy has invented a gadget to hook up **a CD player** / **an MP3 player** in a car.
3. Greg **knows** / **doesn't know** how the gadget works.
4. Jacob knows where Greg can **learn about** / **buy** one.
5. Greg's invention would show your **picture** / **name** every time you log in to a chat room.

Unit 10

A *Track 19* Listen to the conversation on page 102. Todd and Paula are at work.

B *Track 20* Listen to the rest of their conversation. Answer the questions. Check (✓) Todd or Paula.

	Todd	Paula
1. Who will be out of the office tomorrow?	☐	☐
2. Who had a vacation last July?	☐	☐
3. Who's been working on the presentation?	☐	☐
4. Who's going to make copies of the reports?	☐	☐
5. Who's going to read the surveys?	☐	☐
6. Who's going to have a cup of coffee?	☐	☐
7. Who has a lot of work to do by Monday?	☐	☐

Unit 11

A *Track 21* Listen to the conversation on page 112. Debra and Hal are at work.

B *Track 22* Listen to the rest of their conversation. Circle the correct words.

1. Hal's band needs more **practice** / **money**.
2. The band also needs a **drummer** / **singer**.
3. In college, Debra majored in **music** / **accounting**.
4. Debra used to sing **in concerts** / **at parties**.
5. Debra is too **busy** / **tired** to practice on Fridays.
6. Hal thinks Sunday morning is a **good** / **bad** time to practice.

Unit 12

A *Track 23* Listen to the conversation on page 122. Joey and Celia are on the street near Celia's apartment.

B *Track 24* Listen to the rest of their conversation. Choose the right answer. Circle *a* or *b*.

1. Celia left _____ in her car.
   a. some CDs   b. nothing valuable

2. Joey tells Celia a story about their _____ Andrew.
   a. classmate   b. neighbor

3. Andrew's car was stolen from outside a _____ .
   a. gas station   b. store

4. Andrew didn't _____ the car door when he went in to pay.
   a. close   b. lock

5. The police asked for his _____ number.
   a. work phone   b. cell phone

6. When the policeman called the number, the thief told him _____ .
   a. his location   b. his name

SSL3

Unit 1

Alexis Yeah, but she was always saying mean things about her friends. I felt pretty bad for them.

Jacob So, what about your new roommate? What's she like?

Alexis Her name's Kim. She's really nice. Just really friendly.

Jacob That's good. So you get along really well?

Alexis Yeah, . . . but she's pretty talkative. She's always telling me about her work and complaining about her boyfriend.

Jacob Huh. But at least she's not mean.

Alexis No, not mean at all. She really is a nice person. But it's not easy to study when she's home because, you know, her friends are always calling and coming over.

Jacob She sounds incredibly popular.

Alexis Yeah. Actually, she works for an ad agency. So I'm always getting free tickets for concerts and things from her.

Jacob Wow. That's great. So, I guess it's worth listening to all her problems, then.

Alexis Yeah. For sure!

Unit 2

Hal Yeah, me too. What time does it start?

Debra Um . . . it's on at 6:00 and 9:30. If we leave work right at 5:00, we can make the 6 o'clock show.

Hal Yeah, . . . but I haven't finished my report. I won't be ready to leave at 5:00. And what about dinner?

Debra We can get something after the movie. . . .

Hal Well, how about we go at 9:30? It's late, but at least I can finish work, and we can eat.

Debra Maybe there's another movie at 7:00 or 8:00? Let's see. . . .

Hal Oh, I know! Have you seen that new science-fiction movie with Bruce Willis?

Debra No, but I've heard about it. I really like sci-fi.

Hal Do you? Well, see if it's playing someplace.

Debra OK. Oh, look! It's playing at the Plaza tonight!

Hal It is? Perfect. Let's go. What time does it start?

Debra Oh, it starts at 6:30. But you have to finish your report. . . .

Hal Oh, never mind! I'll do it tomorrow.

Unit 3

Kim Can you go camping in Sequoia National Park?

Juan Actually, I'm not sure. But it really is the neatest place.

Kim So, the sequoias there are the tallest trees in the world? How tall are they?

Juan Really tall. They're like a 26-story building!

Kim No way! Really? That's taller than my office building.

Juan And the oldest ones are over 3,000 years old.

Kim They are? That's amazing.

Juan It sure is. Actually, there's one tree that's almost 5,000 years old.

Kim There is? In Sequoia National Park?

Juan No, it's north of Sequoia, in a secret location.

Kim Wow! You really know a lot about trees. Is that your hobby or something?

Juan No, I read all this stuff in my hiking guidebook. You know, the widest trees . . .

Unit 4

Rob Yeah, it seems like families used to be a lot closer.

Paula That's for sure. We used to do everything with my parents when we were kids. We'd always do things together on weekends. We'd go to the park, stuff like that.

Rob Yeah, my dad would play basketball with us. Now it seems like my kids want to do everything with their friends.

Paula Oh, I know. Mine too. I can't even get them to go to a movie with us. They say it's too embarrassing. They just have me drive them everywhere, like I'm the local taxi!

Rob Exactly. Well, maybe you can get them to come over to our house next weekend. We could all have a barbecue. It seems to me that kids are usually interested if there's food – and a pool!

Paula That's true. OK, I'll ask. Thanks, Rob. Oh, I have to get going – the kids want me to take them to the mall!

Unit 5

Laura OK, here's your tea. Be careful. It's hot.

Kayla Oh, thanks.

Laura Are you sure you don't want anything to eat? I have a few homemade cookies left. My mom made them.

Kayla Oh, no, thanks. I'm fine. Really.

Laura Are you sure? They have very few calories. My mom only uses a little sugar, but they're really good. There are some chocolate ones and some ginger ones.

Kayla Well, OK.

Laura Chocolate or ginger?

Kayla Oh! They both look good.

Laura Well, here. Try one of each.

Kayla OK, thanks. Mmm. They're good.

Laura Oh, wait. I have some homemade lemon cake, too. Let me get you some.

Kayla No, really. Maybe later. But do you mind if I have one more ginger cookie? They're so good.

Unit 6

Ling Hi, there. It's me. How was the gym?

Ramon Oh, good. I just got back. How was your seminar?

Ling It was OK. Except I have to go again on Saturday.

Ramon You do? Oh, no. I really wanted to see you.

Ling I know. I'm sorry. But the instructor asked everyone to come to another class on Saturday.

Ramon So did you tell the instructor you have plans for Saturday?

Ling No. I mean, I wanted to say, "I'm meeting my friend," but, well, I couldn't. So much for being assertive, huh!

Ramon Right. Well, you know what? You ought to call the instructor right now and say, "I'm going to have to miss Saturday's class. I have an appointment."

Ling Oh, I can't do that.

Ramon Why not? She'll be impressed with your assertiveness!

Ling You're right. I'll call her and say I can't come. And then I'll call you back.

Ramon Great. Talk to you later. Good luck.

Answer key

Unit 1 1. False 2. True 3. False 4. True 5. False 6. True

Unit 2 1. 6:00 2. before 3. likes 4. Bruce Willis 5. won't

Unit 3 1. a 2. b 3. b 4. a 5. b

Unit 4 1. True 2. False 3. True 4. True 5. False

Unit 5 1. hot 2. Laura's mother 3. sugar 4. ginger 5. likes 6. another cookie

Unit 6 1. False 2. True 3. True 4. False 5. True 6. False

Unit 7

Chen I have one neighbor that I'm pretty friendly with, though, the guy in the apartment across from mine. He's really nice. He helped me move some furniture last month.

Maria Oh, that was nice of him.

Chen Yeah, it was. I've helped him, too. The last time he went away, he gave me a key so I could go in and water his plants.

Maria Yeah? I guess that's the good thing about neighbors – they can help each other out like that.

Chen Yeah, but sometimes it can be a problem, too. Last week, he came back late from a party and couldn't find his key. So, he knocked on my door at 2:00 a.m. and wanted his key back!

Maria At 2:00 a.m.? No way! Well, I guess he had to. . . . It's a little inconsiderate, though. Were you asleep?

Chen Yeah!

Maria Boy. I bet you were mad. Did you complain to him about it?

Chen No. I need him to help me move some more furniture next week!

Unit 8

Nicole Yeah. My aunt and uncle live near Bracken, so it would be a good choice for me. I could live with them – if I go there.

Carlos That would be good.

Nicole Yeah. They have a nice house . . . you know, a lot of rooms, and my aunt makes great food. They used to have a student living with them a few years ago.

Carlos Really? If I were you, I'd go to Bracken next year for sure!

Nicole I know. I'm seriously thinking about it, but I've applied to some other schools, too.

Carlos Yeah? Well, uh, do you think your aunt and uncle might like to have a student living with them this year? I mean, I would pay rent. . . .

Nicole What a good idea! I'll ask them. I'm sure they'll say "Yes."

Carlos Oh, that would be awesome.

Nicole Well, you might want to meet them first. . . . I mean, they're really nice people. My uncle's a big baseball fan. You could go to a game together.

Carlos That would be excellent! Bracken is beginning to sound better already.

Unit 9

Greg Yeah, but take a look. It's a chat room for inventors. . . . I mean, the people on here have made all kinds of things. This one guy has invented a gadget that lets you hook up your MP3 player in the car and play it.

Jacob Huh. I wonder how that works.

Greg I'm not sure how it works, . . . but it's a great idea!

Jacob Actually, I've seen one of those gadgets. I can even tell you where to buy one. Anyway, what are you doing in a chat room for inventors?

Greg Well, actually, I have this idea for an invention. It's software that shows your picture every time you log in to a chat room.

Jacob Huh. I wonder if anyone has thought of that before.

Greg I don't know, but just think – it would be like talking to someone face-to-face! You know what I mean?

Unit 10

Todd Thanks, I will. But wait, won't I see you tomorrow?

Paula No, I'll be out of the office for the rest of the week. I'm going to take a short vacation. I haven't taken a vacation since last July.

Todd Oh, OK. That's good.

Paula Actually, I was wondering if you could finish this presentation for me for Monday. I've been working on it all day, but I haven't been able to finish it yet.

Todd Oh, um . . . all right. Sure.

Paula Oh, and I still haven't made copies of these reports. . . .

Todd OK, I can do that.

Paula Great. And just one more thing, . . . I was wondering if you could read these surveys. I need a report on them by Monday, too.

Todd All right. Um, would it be OK if I asked your assistant for help?

Paula Oh, sorry. She's taking her vacation this week, too – while I'm off. All right. Time for a cup of coffee. Do you want some?

Todd No, thanks. I don't really have time.

Paula OK, well, I'm glad you stopped by. Have a good weekend.

Todd Um, thanks. See you Monday.

Unit 11

Hal Oh, we haven't performed anywhere yet. We're not good enough. We need a lot more practice.

Debra Oh, I see. So, what kind of music do you play?

Hal Well, jazz and some pop music. Actually, we're looking for a singer. We don't have one yet.

Debra You need a singer? Really? I used to sing when I was in college.

Hal Really? I thought you studied accounting.

Debra I did, but I also sang in several music groups. We used to perform at weddings and parties.

Hal You must be pretty good! Would you be interested in joining our band?

Debra Well, I don't know. When do you practice?

Hal Every Friday at 6:00. Are you busy Friday nights?

Debra No, but I couldn't practice then. I'm always so tired at the end of the week. You know what time would be good for me? Sunday morning. Early Sunday morning.

Hal You must be joking! That's one time when we're definitely not available. Uh . . . how about noon instead?

Unit 12

Joey Oh, that's funny. You're lucky that nothing was stolen.

Celia Yeah, well, the thing is, I didn't really have anything valuable inside. Not even any CDs.

Joey Well, that's good. Did you hear about that guy in our class . . . Andrew? His car was stolen.

Celia No, I didn't. What happened?

Joey Well, he was getting gas, and then he went inside to pay, and he left his cell phone in the car. And when he came out, the car was gone!

Celia He didn't lock the car?

Joey No, but the funny thing was, when he went to the police, they asked him for his cell phone number. And then they called it, and guess what? The thief answered the phone!

Celia You're kidding!

Joey No, I'm serious. And then the police officer asked where he was, and the thief told him.

Celia No way! That's hilarious. So, Andrew got his car back?

Joey Yeah. He was lucky.

Illustration credits

Kenneth Batelman: 127, FT-C
Lisa Blackshear: 72, 78
Frank Montagna: 10, 20, 30, 42, 52, 62, 74, 84, 94, 106, 116, 126
Marilena Perilli: x, 7, 19, 32, 37, 47, 64, 88, 89, 101, 108, 128

Tony Persiani: 34, 82, 83
Andrew Vanderkarr: 41, 59, 79, 95, 103, 111
Terry Wong: 3, 31, 49, 91, 98, 110, 119

Photography credits

6, 7, 16, 17 (*top*), **26, 27** (*top row*), **38, 39** (*top*), **40, 44, 48, 49, 54, 58, 59, 70, 71** (*top*), **80, 81, 86, 90, 91, 102, 103, 112, 113** (*top*), **118, 122, 123** (*top*), **SSL1, SSL2, SSL3** ©Frank Veronsky
1 (*clockwise from top left*) ©Punchstock; ©G. Baden/Zefa/Corbis; ©Punchstock; ©Roy McMahon/Corbis
4 (*clockwise from top left*) ©Punchstock; ©Alamy; ©Alamy; ©Punchstock
8 (*clockwise from top left*) ©Peter Kramer/Newscom; ©Chris Polk/AP/Wide World; ©Lori Conn/Newscom; ©Ron Antonelli/Newscom
11 (*clockwise from top left*) ©Alamy; ©Wade Eakle/Lonely Planet Images; ©Franck Prevel/Corbis Sygma; ©Getty Images
12 (*clockwise from top left*) ©Punchstock; ©Steve Prezant/Corbis; ©David Sacks/Getty Images; ©Getty Images
13 ©Darryl Leniuk/Age fotostock
14 (*clockwise from top left*) ©Punchstock; ©Punchstock; ©Alamy
15 ©Hisham Ibrahim/Getty Images
17 (*bottom*) ©Punchstock
18 (*all images*) ©Alamy
19 ©Kate Powers/Getty Images
21 (*top, left to right*) ©Kevin Schafer/Corbis; ©Howard Sayer/Alamy; ©Richard Fisher; (*bottom*) ©Alamy
22 (*clockwise from top left*) ©Wendy Connett/Alamy; ©Aflo Foto Agency/Alamy; Courtesy of Royal Dragon; ©Punchstock; ©Punchstock; ©Age fotostock
23 ©Alamy
24 (*clockwise from top left*) ©Punchstock; ©Nevada Wier/Corbis; ©Galen Rowell/Corbis; ©Age fotostock; ©Fotosearch; ©Mike Blake/Reuters/Corbis
27 (*bottom row, left to right*) ©F. Damm/Zefa/Corbis; ©Sarkis Images/Alamy; ©Bob Kris/Corbis; ©Richard Fisher
28 (*top left*) ©Six Flags/Splash News/Newscom; (*bottom row, left to right*) ©Siegfried Layda/Getty Images; ©AW Photography/Alamy; ©Punchstock
29 ©Hubert Stadler/Corbis
33 (*clockwise from top left*) ©China Tourism Press/Getty Images; ©Ronnie Kaufman/Corbis; ©Punchstock; ©Paul Barton/Corbis
35 ©Punchstock
36 (*clockwise from top left*) ©Kaz Chiba/Getty Images; ©Rob Lewine/Corbis; ©Sharon L. Jonz/PictureQuest; ©Marwan Naamani/AFP/Getty Images
39 (*bottom*) ©Punchstock
40 Courtesy of Rhonda's Ramblings
43 ©George Kerrigan
45 (*left to right*) ©Punchstock; ©Punchstock; ©Andy Crawford/Getty Images
46 (*noodles*) ©Scott Peterson/FoodPix; (*shrimp*) ©James Baigrie/FoodPix; (*vegetables*) ©Punchstock; (*eggs*) ©Thomas Firak/FoodPix; (*potatoes*) ©Robert Brenner/Photo Edit; (*lamb*) ©Punchstock; (*beef*) ©Punchstock; (*raw fish*) ©Marco Cristofori/Corbis; (*smoked fish*) ©Rita Maas/FoodPix
50 (*duk bok gi*) ©John K. Choy; (*samosas*) ©Punchstock; (*falafel*) ©Kathryn Kleinman/FoodPix; (*popcorn*) ©Alamy
51 (*ice cream*) ©Judd Pilossof/FoodPix; (*sticky rice*) ©Thomas Kremer/Stockfood

53 (*left to right*) ©Pedro Coll/Age fotostock; ©SuperStock; ©Christie & Cole/Corbis
61 (*all*) ©George Kerrigan
63 ©David Sacks/Getty Images
65 (*top left*) ©Getty Images; (*all others*) ©Punchstock
66 (*Mike*) ©Ryan McVay/Getty Images; (*Jennifer*) ©Punchstock; (*Toshiro*) ©Punchstock; (*Charlie*) ©Punchstock; (*Angela*) ©Punchstock; (*Christopher*) ©Punchstock
68 (*all*) Kathy Niemczyk
71 (*bottom, left to right*) ©Raoul Minsart/Masterfile; ©Punchstock; ©Punchstock
73 ©Lee Page/Getty Images
75 (*clockwise from top left*) ©Getty Images; ©Motoring Picture Library/Alamy; ©Punchstock; ©Yellow Dog Productions/Getty Images
76 (*clockwise from top left*) ©Chabruken/Getty Images; ©Manfred Rutz/Getty Images; ©Yang Liu/Corbis; ©Punchstock
85 (*clockwise from top left*) ©Masterfile; ©Punchstock; ©Mark Richards/Photo Edit; ©Punchstock
96 ©Punchstock
97 (*clockwise from top left*) ©Punchstock; ©Tom Stewart/Corbis; ©Chuck Savage/Corbis; ©David Leahy/Getty Images
100 (*top row, left to right*) ©Miramax/Newscom; ©MGM/Everett Collection; ©Everett Collection; ©MGM/Newscom; (*bottom row, left to right*) ©20th Century Fox Film Corp/Everett Collection; ©Everett Collection; ©Everett Collection
104 (*Madagascar*) ©DreamWorks SKG/Newscom
105 ©Rick Diamond/Newscom
107 (*clockwise from top right*) ©Punchstock; ©Rana Faure/Getty Images; ©Joe McBride/Getty Images
109 ©Robert Maass/Corbis
113 (*bottom*) ©Punchstock
114 ©Tim DeFrisca/Sports Illustrated
115 (*left to right*) ©Marianne Coates; ©Mark Hyman; Courtesy of The International Book Project
117 (*clockwise from top right*) ©Punchstock; ©Alamy; ©Punchstock; ©David Young-Wolff/Photo Edit
120 (*from left to right*) ©The Reporter/Don Lloyd/AP/Wide World; ©AIN/Reuters/Corbis; ©Punchstock; ©Gaetano Amici/AP/Wide World; ©Matt Black Productions/Gabriel Lee/AP/Wide World
121 ©Punchstock
123 (*bottom*) ©Punchstock
124 Courtesy of OhmyNews
FT-B ©Punchstock
FT-D (*left to right*) ©Chris Fotoman Smith/Alamy; ©Alt-6/Alamy; ©Adrian Weinbrecht/Getty Images
FT-E ©Dex Images/Corbis
FT-G (*left to right*) ©Lee Jae-won/Newscom; ©Armen Asratyan/Newscom
FT-H (*clockwise from top left*) ©Reuters/Corbis; ©Roger Ressmeyer/Corbis; ©C.C. Lockwood/Animals Animals; ©Reuters/Corbis

Text credits

The authors and publishers are grateful for permission to reprint the following items:
40 "Childhood memories" by Rhonda Hutchinson, November 9, 2004. Reprinted by permission.
72 Adapted from "Web site chaperones classmate reunions" by Jefferson Graham, *USA TODAY*. February 2, 2002. Reprinted with permission.
92 Adapted from "Robbing You Blind?" by Carla Fried, *Real Simple*. Copyright © 2004. Time Inc. All rights reserved. Reprinted by permission.
114 Adapted from "Too Good to Be True" by John Garrity, *Sports Illustrated*. October 9, 2000. Copyright © 2000. Time Inc. All rights reserved. Reprinted by permission.
124 Adapted from "A new brand of journalism is taking root in South Korea" by Dan Gillmor. © Copyright. *San Jose Mercury News*. All rights reserved. Distributed by Valeo IP. Reprinted by permission.

Every effort has been made to trace the owners of copyrighted material in this book. We would be grateful to hear from anyone who recognizes his or her copyrighted material and who is unacknowledged. We will be pleased to make the necessary corrections in future editions of the book.

Answers

Unit 3, Lesson A

1 Getting started, Exercise A, page 22

1. b Taipei. Taipei 101 is the tallest office building.
2. a Japan. The Akashi-Kaikyo Bridge is the longest suspension bridge.
3. a Canada. The West Edmonton Mall is the largest shopping mall.
4. b Bangkok. The Royal Dragon is the busiest restaurant.
5. a Rio de Janeiro. Maracanã Municipal Stadium is the biggest soccer stadium.
6. c France.

1 Getting started, Exercise B, page 22

1. What's the <u>biggest</u> train station in the world?   Grand Central Station in New York City. It has the most platforms.
2. What's the <u>busiest</u> airport in the world?   Hartsfield International Airport in Atlanta, Georgia, U.S.A.
3. What's the <u>most expensive</u> city in the world?   Tokyo.